For all the people that grew up in and around a small town,
Wherever it was, but particularly in the South!

Goodwater Goodtimes

A few recollections of some old country boys and
girls growing up in and around a small town.

Compiled and edited by Perry G. Green

Contributors:

Charles Luker

Robert P. Dark

Betty DeGraffenried Burgess

Tommy Dark

Pastor James Long

Perry G. Green

Cover photographs and photography support
Pam Green

Introduction

This is a book of several people's recollections of growing up in and around Goodwater, a small town in Coosa County Alabama. The stories are in no particular order and some are comments on life after Goodwater. They are funny, outrageous, witty and sometimes sad. They reflect the way life was back in a 'better time' and hopefully bring back a few memories and a smile or two. The stories writers are identified by their initials at the end of their tales. There are a few comments and such from others as well. We hope you enjoy these memories and share our love of small town Americana.

The CB

In the early 1960s, my Daddy ran an automotive repair shop in Goodwater, Alabama. We lived in Kellyton which was just seven miles away but in those days it was a long distance phone call from Kellyton to Goodwater. There were no car parts houses in Goodwater so he ordered his parts from Alex City. Since it was not long distance from Kellyton to Alex City he would call my Mom on the CB and give her a list of parts that he needed and she in turn would call the parts house to place the order. We had to save every nickel we could in those days. That's the reason my Daddy had the CB (Citizens Band) radio.

Radios were few and far between back in the early '60s. That was pretty much before the trucking industry discovered them. My Daddy had a couple of them. One at home and one in his 1956 Ford Pick-up. The one in his truck was made by 'HeathKit' and was a large bulky thing and the antenna was a long whip style like Broderick Crawford had on 'Highway Patrol'. Our Federal call sign was '6Q6635'. Earl Evans and Richard Neighbors from Goodwater also had radios and there were some in Alex City. My wayward cousin Tommy Dark got a CB and 'borrowed' our call sign for a short while.

When I was about fifteen or so Daddy would let me drive his pick-up to Methodist Youth Fellowship on Sunday nights. He told me to stay off of the radio but you know what that meant, use it but don't get caught! Well, after church one Sunday night Tommy and I left the church and immediately turned on that CB. We were talking on 'skip' to somebody in Texas (which was totally illegal). Anyway, when we got to the stop sign near the church we saw a fellow who lived on the corner that had a big picture window in his living room.

I just happened to glance toward that big picture window and noticed that as I keyed the microphone his TV went completely bonkers. When I release the microphone his TV straightened back out. Well, guess what little old me and Tommy Dark did next?! We sat there and keyed the microphone on and off. The TV would go crazy and the man that lived there would get up from his chair and walk to the TV to adjust it. There were no remotes back than. Just as he would reach for one of the knobs on the TV I would release the key and the TV would straighten back out.

As soon as he sat back down I would key it again and hold it until he got back up to adjust it. We did this several times and laughed hysterically as the man got up and down. Finally, that man got up one last time and just turned the TV off.

Now for the rest of the story! Quite often on Saturdays when we went home for lunch my dearest cousin Tommy Dark would ride back to Goodwater with us and go to the Saturday afternoon matinee. Mr. Frank Nail operated a movie theater pretty much just across the street from my Daddy's shop. It was mostly Saturday afternoon movies with a few Friday night shows and such. The local theater was one of the few places in town that had air conditioning and it was cool. Sometimes I could go also but most of the time I had to work with my Daddy.

Once I heard Mr. Nail tell my Daddy that occasionally his CB radio transmissions would somehow block the sound of the movie and that everything being said on the CB could be heard loud and clear in the theater. That radio had two transmit channels and Daddy discovered that it only bled into the theater on channel eleven. Therefore, if he needed to call for parts he would use the other channel on Saturdays in order to not disturb the theater patrons.

Well, armed with this knowledge of what channel eleven would do to the theater sound system I would wait until I figured the movie had been going about thirty minutes or so. I would then make sure Daddy was busy working on something. When the coast was clear I would sneak out to the truck, turn the CB to channel eleven, key the microphone and say, "Tommy Dark to the lobby, Tommy Dark please come to the lobby". It would completely override the sound coming from Dracula or whatever movie was showing.

I was only able to do this a couple of times before Mr. Nail paid another visit to my Daddy. Needless to say, that ended my theater announcement days and I am not sure that I was ever able to even attend another movie in Goodwater. Fun days for sure. It didn't take much to entertain us in those days. We were mischievous as all boys can be but we never got into any real trouble. Except for my cousins propensity for stealing Buicks but that's another story! RD

Shooting Craps

This story is to point out what an innocent rascal Tommy Dark was. We always found a way to entertain ourselves and we never really intended for it to be criminal or wrong as we did things just for fun! When I was a sophomore and Tommy was a senior in high school there was a covert gambling scheme that was being practiced by 99.9% of all the male students. It was not a very big thing as most of us didn't have much money but it was entertaining and fun. Matching coins (odd or even) and shooting high dice were the most popular games. You could match coins all day and at the end of the day you would most likely still have your twenty cents! Odds were 50-50! Shooting high dice was practiced by the boys that had more coins to play with. Not 'craps' where you have to shoot a seven or eleven or some such but just the 'high' dice!

Anyway, after a few weeks it was pretty common knowledge what was going on and who was involved. We were notified that we were having an after school meeting in a certain class room. We knew better than to not attend so we all gathered in that room. Then in steps Mr. C. O. Westbrook (COW) our principal. He was doing his job as always. He had gotten a list from somewhere of all the guilty parties and that included those watching! Also in attendance were Mr. George White, Coach Gene Hayes and Coach James Hayes all standing at attention and on guard. I might add that this was the time for penny loafers, cordovan in color!

Mr. COW, and I say that respectful, started the meeting to inform us of our guilty charges (no trial necessary, thank you very much) and then preceded to tell us how our parents could go to jail for our misbehavior. Then he started his long lecture about being disappointed and unhappy with our gambling and shooting 'craps.' He was totally involved in this lecture and repeatedly referred to shooting 'craps.' When the lecture was at its most intense moment Tommy Dark slides out of his desk and starts his TD shuffle sliding in his cordovan penny loafers toward the door to leave. Mr. COW asked rather firmly, "Where are you going Tommy?" Tommy returns the look and with a half smile informs Mr. COW that he had not been shooting 'craps.' Mr. COW asked rather sternly "Well, what have you been doing?" Tommy informed Mr. COW that he had been shooting 'high dice.' Lordy, I thought I would wet my pants. I don't know what took place with TD and Mr. COW but I can only assume it wasn't good for Tommy! CL

The Stolen Buick

My cousin Robert Dark said stories need to be short because people lose interest. I couldn't help it with this one. I had to tell everything. I started driving vehicles when I was very young. By age twelve I could operate most anything including tractors. In those days I would drive the old Kellyton roads often as police were seldom if ever seen.

One fall day when I was a student at Goodwater High School we got out early for a teachers meeting. Gary Shivers (Big G) and myself rode the bus that day and we both decided to tell the driver to let us off at my dad's shop. We had no plan other than goofing off the rest of the day. It was 1962 and I did not yet have my driver's license as I had just turned fifteen. Gary had his but we did not have a car to ride in. It was during my dad's lunch hour so the shop was closed. I told Gary I guess we would just wait until they opened back up to see what our next move would be.

As we were walking around to the back side of the shop I noticed a nice looking car pulled up to one of the shop doors. There sat a shiny yellow and white 1956 Buick. I told Gary I had never driven a big Buick so get in. He suggested that I let him drive being as he already had turned sixteen and had his license. I said no way! It would be no problem as the police probably thought I was sixteen anyway. I never even thought of why this car was at my dad's shop. I started it up and I told Gary this thing is skipping but we are going for a ride anyway. I pulled out on 280 heading for the ride of a lifetime as we were now riding in a Buick! I told Gary how nice this car drove. We both felt like a million dollars riding down 280.

I had not travelled far and all of sudden I noticed a State Trooper. I told Gary I would just turn into the trailer park and we would be fine. My heart was beating a little faster though. After sitting for about twenty minutes in the trailer park I got calm again. I told Gary I guess we need to get this car back to the shop as my dad would soon be returning from lunch soon. He kept telling me to let him drive and I said the Trooper would be gone and all would be good.

I pulled out on 280 heading back to the shop. I guess I went about a half mile and Gary told me I might want to look in the mirror. Lo and behold that same Trooper was on my tail. I was now in full panic. I asked Gary if he could swap with me while we were driving but we soon discovered that would not work.

I turned on the road that would take me to downtown Kellyton and guess what ? The trooper also turned. Now I knew things were not going to be good for old Tom.

He put the blue light on me just as I was about to make the left turn heading back to the shop. Now my heart was beating about 200 mph. Gary was sort of laughing but not me. The trooper walked up to my side and asked to see my license. I told him I did not have one. He asked how old I was and I told him fifteen. He then begin to question me on who's car I was driving. I paused a second and said I didn't know. That's when things got a little scary. He told me to come back to his car and have a seat. Gary was in tears laughing at me but I was not very amused.

The trooper got on his radio and made some calls. He asked me did I steal the car and I said no. He looked at me like boy are you nuts. He said, "Now let me get this correct, Dark. You have no license, you don't know who's car this is and you want me to believe all this?" I told him the car was being worked on at my dad's shop. I didn't even know that for sure but had to think quick. He asked who my dad was and I told him. He ran a check on the car and it had not been reported stolen but things were still not adding up. I don't think I ever seen a trooper so mad as his face was a full red color. He asked me if we could call my dad and I told him no way, that he would kill me. He told me, "Son, I should just take you to jail but for now I am just going to give you a ticket." I really think the trooper was laughing under his breath but he acted mean.

He then asked Gary if he had a license and of course he did. The trooper said for Gary to drive the car to my dad's shop and for me to stay in the passenger seat and not move. He said he was going to follow us and I had better not be telling a lie.

Just as Gary started driving the Buick here comes Uncle Charlie. I thought oh no, Pop is soon to follow. We pulled the Buick in at the shop with the state trooper following close behind. Uncle Charlie was raising the shop doors. I rushed over to him and pleaded for him not to tell my dad. I needed to live a few more years I said. He replied he would not tell but got on me pretty hard for taking a car they were working on. I promised I had learned my lesson. At least for now I was out of trouble but not to worry.

My uncle Charlie told me the car was in the shop because the engine had two pistons shot and he had let it sit there so the engine could cool while he was eating lunch.

I told him no wonder I could never get it above 50 mph. It's a good thing the engine was bad or I would probably have ended up in jail for speeding and grand theft auto! I do not have clue who owned the Buick. All I know is it was one of my dads customers. I sure am glad the owner never found out or I would have been in deep trouble. Then again I worked at the shop part time so it was not really stealing, right? I was only testing it out.

Now I had to figure out how in the world I was going to pay the fine. I had to be quite about what had happened so I could not ask anyone for the money. I sure didn't have any money at the time. My plan came in place a few days later after my parents had gone to bed. I had thought for several days on how I would come up with the money. My dad always had a very large billfold and I remember him always having lots of cash. While they were sleeping I crawled on the floor to the hallway where my dad put his things. I slowly reached up and got a twenty dollar bill out and put everything back like it was. I think it took over an hour sliding across the floor and back to my bed but I pulled off the job and nobody woke up. At the time I felt bad about getting the $20 from my dad but I weighed all the options. I had always planned on paying him back but I just couldn't do it while I was still living at home. I kept this a secret for almost five years. Whew, I was now ready to pay the fine.

The problem now was I had no car or drivers license and could not take the chance of getting caught again anyway. I told my mother I needed to go to Alex City to buy a present for somebody. She asked me who and I told her I had to keep it a secret. While she shopped in downtown Alex City I ran across the street to where all the fines were paid. It was an old building across and down from Carlisle Drug store.

I walked in and told the lady who I was and what I had to do. The little old lady told me to have a seat that the judge would see me in a while. I was scared that I was not going to have enough money to pay the fine so panic set in again. Finally after what seemed like a lifetime a man who looked to be at least 100 years old came up to me and said I understand you are the one that was driving in Kellyton in a stolen car with no drivers license. I thought Oh No, this is it for me. I would be sent to jail for a long time.

He finally told me the fine would be $17.50. I will remember that amount until I die. I give them the $20 bill and got my change and started to leave and the Judge told me to hold on one second.

I thought oh no now what? He went on to tell me how light I got off. He said he knew all the Darks and they were all good people and for me to not mess up the family name anymore. Whew, I was then clear to go. I had learned my lesson and like always the hard way.

I was home on leave from the Air Force in 1967 and finally told my mother and father about what happened that day in 1962. I was on my own then and I knew it was safe to tell. My mom and dad both laughed and then my dad looked at me and said, "Boy, what were you thinking?" I told him I was not sure. He then told me to pay him the $17.50 and add $2.50 for me stealing it. I forked over the $20 and we all laughed about it the rest of the day. My dad made sure he got his money back. I miss sharing my stories with them. I only wish I could have had them with me for a few more years but that was not to be. The both passed away too young. Not many things did I ever pull over on my parents but this one I did with success.

I look back and wonder how I survived all the stress I was facing wondering what they were going to do to me. I think like two weeks passed before I got the money to pay the fine. For a fifteen year old I can tell you I was worried and I guess that was my punishment. I never told anyone and Gary kept his promise to be quite of which I am glad and of course my Uncle Charlie. I thanked Uncle Charlie years later for saving me that day. I am sure the punishment would not have been good for me! TD

Halloween Lights

In the 1950s I don't remember getting a costume for Halloween but I do remember walking all over town with my friends carrying a grocery sack to fill with candy. The most special place was Miss Patti Fleming's house. As I recall she always had very special treats and maybe even some hot chocolate for us. We were lucky to get a small piece of candy anywhere else.

However, the most memorable Halloween for me occurred in 1959, I think, when I was a junior in high school. By this time, of course, I was too old for trick or treating but I was still out and about on Halloween night. Before the night ended however I was hauled down to the police department! Rose Buttram and Joe Broom were dating and Joe went to high school in Sylacauga. He had a friend named James Gray who had gone to school in Goodwater in the first and second grade. James had a pretty convertible which was white with red interior, I think. They asked me to go out riding with them and I did. Some of the Goodwater boys were riding around town that night shooting out street lights with BB guns. I'm not sure who all was involved but I think Billy Ray Hatley was one of the culprits and I wouldn't be surprised if Jimmy Sharman and Mike Swindall were involved as well. As I recall there were quite a few of them stirring up mischief that night. They were also scaring some of the younger kids who were going door to door unchaperoned getting Halloween candy. Anyway, either Joe or James also had a BB gun and decided to get in on the fun so one of them shot out one street light.

Almost immediately we were stopped by the local police and hauled down to the police station! James and Joe were blamed for all of the damage that had been done all over town mainly by others. I think James' fancy car with a sixty-one license plate for Talladega County and not a twenty-two for Coosa County attracted our local policeman's attention as they wanted to capture the outside agitators. Fortunately, Rose and I were not forced to go into the station but stayed in the car and cried. Somehow Mr. Buttram was called down there to get us and he took me home and went inside to tell Mama what had happened. I think the boys got off with just paying a small fine and paying to have all the streetlights replaced. The local boys, I'm sure, were very proud of themselves for never getting caught. I never saw James Gray again! BDB

The Prophet, Charles Luker and going to Hell.

I became a member of Kellyton First United Methodist Church in 1979. There was something I realized about that church from the very beginning. It was almost like having a Goodwater High School reunion every Sunday. There was Larry Shivers and Peggy, Jerry Newberry and Charlotte Shivers Newberry, Steve Culberson, Rick Durden and Dawn Culberson Durden, Robert Butch Dark, Tim Dark and Cathy Andrews Dark, Gary Shivers and Judy, Mickey Melton and Sherry Shivers Melton, John, Ed and Ann Gilliland, Todd Hayes and Lynn Lawley Hayes, Dale Burns and Teresa Hayes Burns, James and Linda Baird, Donna Dark Patterson, Bill Dark and Janice Bruce Dark, Mike Powell and Deborah Powell, Ricky Ayres and Sandra Powell Ayres, Mike Howard and Susan, Charles and Melinda Luker, Billy Humphry and Patty Osborn Humphrey, Melanie Catchings Mosley, Chris and Denise Dark, James and Dian Long and a bunch of old folks. Some of these left for different reasons. Some moved on to better jobs in different cities, some for better schools, some divorced, etc. The active list would change but you get the idea. For some reason I feel that I'm forgetting someone but not intentionally.

Brother Mike Jackson came to the church in June of 1998. He and his wife was Connie were such a blessing. The two of them kept things very lively and were not afraid to try new things to awaken the congregation to the Holy Spirit. Then there came the Sunday service I will never forget. Brother Mike was well into the message when suddenly the door opened with a loud report. Every head turned and every eye looked to see what was going on. Then and there The Prophet of God entered.

She was dressed in a long white robe and in her hand she held a shepherds staff about seven foot long with a large hook on the end. She raised the staff above her head as if she was Moses himself. By this time I was thinking what is Connie Jackson up to this time? I thought this was part of Brother Mikes program and message. Sister Moses strolls up the center of the church and points her staff at Charles Luker and says, "You are going to Hell!"

It was at this moment that everyone knew she must be a Prophet of God because she knew Charles so very well. However, Charles was the only one who realized that this was not a part of the worship service. Charles jumped to his feet and said, "Maybe so but you are going out the door now!"

Charles threw the woman and her staff out the door. The very next week Charles was removed from the welcoming committee! I understand that very same day The Baptist Church of Kellyton was paid a visit from Sister Moses! It seems that she knew some of them as well as she knew Charles. This is just another reason to go to church on Sunday, something exciting is always happening in the house of the Lord. God Bless. JL

Charles relates the following as he remembered that day. Seeing as she had her hand under her cloak I didn't know if she had a gun! We welcomed anyone and everyone to our church but that was certainly not the way to make an entry. The funny thing is about a year before this she was working on her Master's Degree and was needing information about timber land in Coosa County. I told her the listing was $150 and she said she didn't have the money to pay for it as she was in college and trying to write this paper. She was not begging by any means and old compassionate Charlie told her he would take care of it! I did! Another female was with her that day but she stayed outside. I think she visited several churches that day. Lou Jean Cannon says she visited Goodwater Baptist a few times as well. She understood she had some mental problems. Her family helped her get some help and she is now a very nice and important part of trying to improve our City and surrounding areas.

The Christmas Tree

Growing up we never had a 'bought' Christmas tree and certainly never one of those fake aluminum things that were popular at one time and may still be for all I know. We did have Christmas trees but they were ones we (read I) went out into the woods around the house and gathered. Now this was not a one time go into the woods and find a tree thing.

I was hunting Christmas trees all year long. When I would go squirrel hunting or duck hunting or just wandering around in the woods looking for treasures I was always keeping an eye out for the perfect tree. The treasures are still out there by the way if anyone is interested! A mental note would be made of the trees location and filed away. I needed several trees as there was one for the house and one for Grannie and one for who knows might need one, for a small fee of course! Now most of these trees were not on our property although some were. It mattered not as whoever owned the land would not know that one of their trees was missing (hopefully)!

A few other items I would keep an eye out for were holly trees as you could make a decent wreath with it and it was cheap. The big problem with holly was that the leaves had these sharp sticker edges on them and had to be handled rather carefully. I think I still have a few scars here and there from harvesting them! Also my mother worked at the cotton mill during this time and she would bring home these empty conical thread spools and they would be laid out in a circle, pointed end inside on a cardboard base and painted silver, green or red and accented with the holly and a few bows and such. Real nice and again the price was right.

Mistletoe was also a biggie but it was fairly common all around the area. Most oak trees had some growing up in the branches. One could climb up there and dislodge it or more often just shoot it out with one of the many guns we had around the house. People would actually pay for a nice sprig of mistletoe during the yule season. There it was all over the place yet you could get a quarter for a nice sprig in town with no problem. Like taking Christmas candy from a baby!

The tree was placed in a left over can with some dirt and it was watered regularly at least I was supposed to. No store bought tree holder thingies for us as that cost money and well you know! The tree was placed in the appropriate area and then decorated.

There were a few ornaments left over from the previous year that we had managed to not break and the ubiquitous tinsel stuff that you could still find remnants of here and there even in July! Then those lights. These were usually red, white and blue if my part timers is letting the right memory come through. Now these things were wired in series which meant that if one light went out they all went out! The trick was to find out which one. The lights when bought came with a few extra bulbs and you could buy replacements if you needed some. Nowadays you just buy a whole new string. So one by one you had to remove a light and replace it with a new one until they came on again. If perchance you had an old bad replacement bulb that had not been thrown away previously you could be there all day! I learned a few choice words watching my father do this once!

The gifts were placed under the tree as they came in. My relatives would sent us presents as would we to them. I noticed a curious thing one day. The relatives had sent some presents and they were in their rightful place under the tree but lo (lo, a not oft used word) my mother's presents had the same paper on them as did the presents we had wrapped at home. They were decidedly different from the wrapping paper that the relatives had used! I pointed out this discrepancy and she was busted! Seems she just could not wait till Christmas eve when we opened presents. Opening presents on Christmas eve left room under the tree for Santa to leave stuff as we slept.

As I mentioned I was supposed to water this tree every day and I did when I thought about it. Now even back then they had public service announcements about watering your tree and I was all up in there with that till I smelled the hot cocoa but that's another story! Fortunately none of them ever caught fire even with those lights that would get so hot as to leave a mark if you got too close for whatever reason. Being the skeptic that I was even back then I had to see for myself if what they had said about the trees blazing up were true or if they were just blowing smoke. A 'sperment was in order.

We (read I) took the tree down and recovered the ornaments that had survived another season and took off the lights that were no longer working anyway and took the tree out into the yard. Now you could never remove all that tinsel sh. . .uh. . .stuff so it became a casualty of The Great Christmas Tree Fire as it is referred to in the family lore! I will leave it to the readers imagination as to the results as it is still somewhat painful to recall! PGG

Fetchin' Water, A Big Stick and a Mean Dog

Although the account of this story is not first hand information, it came from my Daddy, so it has to be the Gospel. I had two cousins named Bill and Ed Dark. They were the sons of my Dad's oldest brother, Sam. Those boys were operating bulldozers long before they were old enough to have a driver's license. They were very good at what they did and everyone in the surrounding areas knew it.

It seems that in their younger days, they were in the process of building a pond for a gentleman on his farm. It was during the hot, humid typical Alabama summertime and even if you had water it soon got hot and went flat. It was still drinkable but not very refreshing. Sometime about mid-morning as the sun was getting high and the temperature was rising the boys decided to go to the farmer's house for some 'fresh' water. Ed volunteered he would go fetch them some cool water and bring it back for their relief.

As he approached the farmhouse he noticed a BIG old dog that had a menacing look on his face. That dog was watching every move that Ed made. Ed cautiously walked to the door and knocked. When the lady of the house came to the door Ed asked if he could get some fresh cool water for him and his brother. She readily agreed. Then he asked the lady, "Will that dog bite"? The lady said, "He won't bite unless you walk up to him with a stick in your hand. For some unknown reason he goes completely crazy and tries to eat you alive. Be thankful you didn't have a stick when you walked over here". Ed got the water and the boys went back to work.

Later that afternoon, the boys took another break and decided that they needed some more cool, fresh water. Ed told Bill that it was his turn to go fetch the water this time. Ed said to his brother, "Bill, they have a great big old mean looking dog down there. The lady told me that as long as you got yourself a big stick that the dog would leave you alone". Well, Bill got himself a big stick and headed towards the farmhouse. He almost didn't make it out alive. That dog came at him like a freight train with his lips peeled back and in the full 'eat-you-alive' mode. I will leave it to the readers imagination as to the discussions that occurred later between Bill and Ed! RD

A Man Named Clyde

When Melinda and I brought the property we now live on I acquired a rather unique situation. An old man came with the property! It's really a shame that he did not write a book about his life as it would have been entertaining. His biggest obstacle in doing so was he couldn't read or write. I think everyone within a thirty mile radius of our home knew Clyde Worthy. I don't guess he had a profession other than making "moonshine", bird hunting, playing baseball and residing in Kilby Prison. For those that don't know Kilby was the State Prison in Montgomery. It was near where the Coliseum is now. There is currently a shopping area that sits on that old prison site as it was torn down many years ago.

Anyway, when we bought the property Clyde approached me and he had a mouth full of snuff. He inquired as to what was his situation now as he had built a one room cabin on the property and he was in his eighties. I told Clyde that we were not going to ask him to leave and he could live in his cabin or the block house on the other side of the road as long as he wished. In his way of thanking me he asked me if I wanted a good drink of liquor and produced a pint of moonshine that had snuff almost all the way down to the bottom of the bottle. I thanked him but I told him if I ever wanted a drink I would ask him. He smiled! I don't know if it was because I didn't drink his liquor or that he knew he had a place to hang his hat for the rest of his life that made him smile. Perhaps both.

I have several stories about Clyde but I will tell one that Robert Culberson told me about the Kellyton baseball team. Many years ago a lot of communities had baseball teams that played each other and they were hotly contested most of the time as it was a source of community pride. This particular game was to be played against Kilby Prison in Montgomery and Kilby had a really good team and Kellyton wanted to beat them. Someone suggested they asked Clyde, who was not in prison at the time, if he would be their pitcher. Clyde was a great pitcher with a super curve ball. The discussion got to the point that they were concerned that Clyde might start a fight if Kellyton got behind in the game! Also there was the chance that he might know some of the convicts that may not have enjoyed Clyde while he had been living there. They did ask him and Clyde indicated that he would behave just to get to pitch in the game.

The arrangements were in placed and the team loaded on a bus for the trip to Kilby Prison with Clyde sitting in the front seat like a promising citizen! Snuff and all!

When the bus arrived on the Kilby campus the Kellyton players noticed for the first time all the barbed wire they were going to have to go through to get to the playing field that held several hundred convicts. Carefully the bus parked in the place as directed by the guards so the players could unload the bus. Clyde was the first one off and entered the secured area and there was a good bit of noise and hollering going on as Clyde entered the area. Frightened at first, the Kellyton players didn't know whether to run and get back on the bus or what. Then they noticed that most of the convicts knew Clyde and seemed glad to see him again. They were patting him on the back and I guess he held a brief press conference. After all, Clyde was quiet an ambassador. He was a sight and I think he wore overalls to play in and had a can of snuff close by to settle his nerves. Not sure if he had any 'shine and didn't ask. Clyde was about 5' 6" and weighed about 135 pounds soaking wet! He was some character that had few chances at a good life but I guess he was happy! I was privileged to have know him and my life would have been much less without him in it. CL

FFA

My brother Charles started GHS in the fall of 1958. I was eleven years old at the time and loved to follow Charles any place he went. How else was I going to learn things! We had two barns on our property and Charles wanted to get a cow being as he had joined the Future Farmers of America (FFA). I had no desire to work on a farm so this was not my cup of tea. Charles gets the cow and now he has to make sure the cow is fed everyday. This was getting on my nerves because he was spending less time with me so I needed to come up with a plan to stop this madness.

My grandfather had told me how hard farm work was so farming was not in my plan but it was for my brother. Everyday he would get out of school, grab something to eat and feed that dang cow. I wanted to do other things but this cow had to be taken care of. My plan had now come into place.

I would sneak up to the old barn and hide in the woods. Then when Charles would come to feed the cow I would scare him. He would then sell the cow and go back to playing basketball or ping pong with me. At least that was the plan and the plan was on.

The days had grown short and darkness came quickly after school so hiding would not be a problem. Charles went to feed the old cow and I hid in the bushes out of sight. I started making loud wolf like sounds and I knew he would be spooked. Maybe then he would sell the cow. I forgot one thing about this so called well thought out plan.

When Charles kept hearing those wolf sounds he found an old Coke bottle and threw it in the direction the sounds were coming from. The back of my head took a direct hit and I let out a scream like that you would hear in the movies or something. Blood was coming from everywhere.

Soon Charles figured out it was me instead of the big bad wolf and he came running. He took off to the house to get help. I managed to get up and make it home but I was losing blood quick. My mother loaded me up in the car and off to the hospital we went. I was thinking what in the world was happening?

The doctor stitched on the back of my head for about an hour. The doctor had asked me how this happened and in fear of getting my brother in trouble I told him I had fell on a rock while running. I don't remember what ever happened to the cow but I do know I never tried that trick again! TD

Loose in the Caboose

Growing up as I did we never took any of our cars or other mechanical thingies to the garage or wherever people took things like that to get them fixed. We did it ourselves. Had no other option. Those garage things cost money and as there was a severe lack of the same in our general vicinity we had to do it ourselves. Also we didn't go to Auto Zone or some such for parts, we went to whatever junkyard had a car similar to the one we were working on to cannibalize parts. Even searched a few trash piles on occasion for tires that had a few more miles left in them for the old pickup but that's another story. I learned a lot watching, holding wrenches and helping bleed brakes and such. Remember somebody asking me once many years later why I knew how to work on a car. My answer was simple, "I grew up poor!"

Used to help my Dad and Uncle Wolf and others work on cars and learned a whole new language that I had never heard before. Even embarrassed a few sailors once after I joined the Marines! I can't think of any pain much worse that your hand slipping on a wrench in freezing temps and hitting your knuckles on whatever is in your hands path. Much screaming and gnashing of teeth. Right up there with hitting your finger with a hammer or some such in the same conditions. To this day I refuse to work on anything mechanical if it is below about sixty degrees! Did not have that luxury way back then though.

Dad had built a garage (sorta) to do this work in. The walls were less than airtight and the wind could whip thru there like nobody's business. At least it had a roof and it didn't leak so that was something. The only problem with this arrangement was that the cars refused to break down in the yard. They were usually a few miles or more away and a tow truck was out of the question due to that money shortage thing in our general area. This meant they had to be pulled back to the house with a rope or chain or whatever was handy. This operation required two people, one to do the pulling and one to steer the afflicted vehicle. The one in the rear also had the responsibility to apply the brakes to prevent a rear end collision from occurring.

On this particular occasion my Uncle's car, a 1948 Ford sedan if my part timers isn't messing with me, had broken down not far from the house and he was anxious to get it to the garage and fix it. There being no other available individuals around I was recruited. I was about ten at the time and being the automotive genius I was at the time readily agreed. Now I had to sit on a pillow to see (kinda) over the dashboard and could not reach the brake pedal but I was not deterred. Neither was my Uncle who should have known better but I don't remember a whole lot of thought going into this particular rescue mission. Fortunately the tow was all pretty much uphill so braking would not be problem.

The towing vehicle was positioned and a rope was tied to the offending Ford and all was set. I was in position and my Uncle had given me my final instructions which consisted of 'Follow me'! It was on! We start out slowly and all is going according to plan. I am following at the full extent of the rope and it is tight as it should be. I can see well enough and I follow not like I had much of a choice but I was doing well. Staying between the ditches as it were. Then it happened! The rope broke! I did mention we were going mostly uphill which was to our advantage didn't I? Well, not so much now. I started going backwards. While a 1948 Ford does have a rear window it is not made to look out of, it is mostly for decoration. That's why it has mirrors on both sides. Funny I had never noticed them before. Plus everything in a mirror is backwards anyway. Not to worry as I am only going backwards very slowly. Well at first. Then I start picking up speed. Brakes are out of the equation so I do the only thing I can do, I just hang on for dear life! Fortunately the car eases into the passenger side ditch and the side of the car contacts the bank which acts as brake to slow the vehicle down and stop my descent. Didn't do much for the paint job and esthetics on that side not that I cared but my Uncle was less than pleased.

"What happened?' he cried. All I could say was, "I was loose in the caboose!" PGG

Bush Hooking!

A few of us in our younger days and our not so younger days caught a lot of fish on Hatchet and Weogufka Creek by bush hooking. It is what it sounds like. We would wade and swim down the creeks and tie nylon lines about thirty inches long on over hanging bushes along the creek. It was a pretty hard job but it was really enjoyable. We started out by preparing the line and hooks in which I had probably 250 but usually we limited it to 100 hooks per creek side. Bait was always an issue but we used cut chicken livers, salted minnows, ivory soap, catalpa worms, etc. We usually baited most of our hooks before we started our journey down the creek and we draped the hooks around our necks for easy access. We tied our hooks to the overhanging bushes but we would first grab the bush and gave it a good snatch to get the snakes off, REALLY!

We always tied our hooks out as close to nightfall as we could as this would eliminate bream from taking the baits off. Occasionally, if we had a crew of three or four we would put in a few trot lines across the creek in order to help increase our catch. Getting to the end of the trip down the creek we would usually hop up on the bank and walk back to our vehicle and at times that was a tough trip. Briars, tangled bushes and snakes usually kept us on our toes.

At times we would camp out or sleep in our vehicles such that we could get our hooks and fish very early in the morning. Our meal preparation for the trip was usually very simple and consisted of a pound of wieners, a bag of buns and a bottle of catsup. This allowed us to create great hot dogs and if we had any left we might have them for breakfast. The next morning was a treat to behold to look down the creek and see the bushes jiggling around with the catch. The early morning fog rising from the creek increased the anticipation of our early morning plunge into the creek. We usually would wear old boots and old blue jeans as creek walking can be tough on your feet and shins! The jeans and boots were really refreshing the next morning as they were still wet and cold but as soon as we got in the creek the temperature equalized.

Our purpose now was to gather all of our hooks whether they had fish on them or not as we would use the hooks and lines many times. Fish were usually pretty active while on the lines and it was always exciting to take a fish off of your hook and place them on the stringer attached to your belt loop.

It was discouraging to approach a line anticipating a fish on it and find a cotton mouth having had swallowed your fish. Usually, I left that hook for someone else! After securing all of our hooks and fish we usually started the task of cleaning the fish and using the creeks fresh water to rinse them. If we caught five fish or fifty-five the trip was always a success because it was a memory that you would never forget and another friendship forged for life.

I have bush hooked with quiet a few folks and it has to be a memory they cherish, too. Some of the places we fished were the Dam, the railroad trestle, Kings Bridge, Lawson Mill bridge, head of the backwater of Hatchett, Perkins Camp, Hoss Stomp, Big Bend, Whirlpool Hole, Blue Hole, Bill Mann's Cabin, Forks of the Creek, Socapatoy Creek, Swamp Creek, Weoka Creek, Elkahatchee Creek, Big Bend and many others. These are places that I think about at times and it always brings a smile and a great memory as those were things that make you happy now. Some of the peoples names include Estes, Carr, Mask and father, Hyde, Conaway, Neighbors, Dowdle, Floyd and others but all of them are special. The campfires, the hot dogs, grilled chicken, sleeping in the outdoors and yes, an occasional steak are memories that I still hold close to my heart and memory. CL

Sherbet Push-ups, Green Plums and Whuppin's

Back in the mid 1950s, I was in the second grade at that little rock schoolhouse in Kellyton, Alabama. The first and second grades were together in one room and we had the same teacher for both grades. Mrs. Dickenson was her name and what a lovely lady she was. She gave me my first school whuppin' (one of hundreds) when I was in the first grade for putting a crayon on the pot-bellied stove used to warm the classroom. That was a stinking mess that smoked up the entire classroom.

In those days we had some of the most wonderful hot lunches served in a separate old wooden building. It was real food and those lunchroom ladies put their heart and soul into making sure it was the best that it could be. We all looked forward to the Wednesday lunch because we would get a dessert of either an ice-cream sandwich, a Popsicle or one of those new fangled sherbet push-ups. We all really liked the push-ups. After lunch we usually had a short play period before going back to class.

One Wednesday we were finishing up our push-ups on the playground and Mike Ogburn was leaning against that old rock building working on the last few slurps of his sherbet. My delinquent cousin Tommy Dark, myself and one more fellow had finished ours and for some unknown reason we threw the empty cardboard containers at Mike. He told us to stop and leave him alone. Well, that was the wrong thing to say. We ran over to the edge of the playground and each of us stripped a handful of green plums from the bushes in the area and ran back over to where Mike was and started bombarding him with green plums. When we ran out of plums we started throwing small rocks which is where the trouble started.

A rock hit Mike in the mouth and snapped off one of his front teeth. The rest of that day will live on in infamy. Mike told Mrs. Dickinson that it was me who had thrown the life changing stone. I don't remember what happened to Tommy and the other fellows but the rest of my day went something like this: Mike's mother was called and she carried him to the dentist. I got a whuppin' from Mrs. Dickinson. After that I was sent to the Principal's office where I got another whuppin'. Then my Mama was called and when I got home I got a "sho-nuff circle-whuppin'." A circle whupin' is when whoever is administering the punishment holds on to one of your hands and you dance in a circle trying to get away!

When Daddy came home from work I got another whuppin'. Times were different in those days. If you got a paddling in school your parents knew about it before you got home that afternoon. There must have been an unwritten state law in those days that required parents to give their kids another flogging if they got one in school. I think they called it 'corporal punishment'. Last time I looked a Corporal represented a military person that had little clout. Most of my whuppin's could have been called 'Eisenhower Punishments' cause he was a five star general!

Later that night, Mike's daddy called my daddy and wanted to know if he could come over and give me another whuppin'? Daddy told him that he thought I had learned the error of my ways and that additional floggings were unnecessary.

Mike turned sixty-seven last December and as far as I know he doesn't have a cavity in his head. However he has a partial plate with one tooth on it because of something that happened in the second grade. He still says it was me who threw the rock but I think that Tommy was the culprit. Yeah, Tommy! I'm sticking with that!
RD

Old South!

When I was about ten or eleven years old my cousin Scotty and I played baseball in some form almost everyday. A lot of days we played in Mr. Major Andrews yard as it was bigger and it was next door to the Darden's Home. Ms. Martha had some little dogs that barked at us all the time we were playing. We would eventually wind up throwing rocks at them making them bark louder and more aggressively. I think she believed it was Scotty who was doing all of the rock throwing and aggravating of the dogs as she never showed a lot of love toward him or so it appeared to me.

That's what brought me to the statement the Old South. One week Ms. Darden had one of her nephews to come visit her from Arizona and I am pretty sure he was bored. Anyway, Ms Darden called my mama and requested that I come and play with the Darden lad and my mama said that I would be glad too! I was not mad but rather confused because I didn't know anything about folks from Arizona! On the appointed day I was to go everything bad that could happen to a little boy during the summer happened to me. I had to take a bath and wash behind my ears, put on a shirt, clean shorts and even shoes. I didn't have to worry about combing my hair as I had a fresh GI haircut a few days prior. I walked to the Darden home and as I stepped into the yard I saw cousin Scotty and someone else playing pitch with a baseball.

I knocked on the door and Ms. Martha answered and welcomed me. She then introduced me to her kin and we shook hands and I noticed Ms. Martha smiling at the gesture. First Ms. Martha served us cookies and cold lemonade that was really good. I can remember sitting on her front porch watching the condensation roll down my cold glass of lemonade. After refreshments, I asked if he would like to play something like pitch with a baseball and before he could answer Ms. Martha answered inside the door that Johnny (or whatever his name was) doesn't want to play ball. "Yes Mam", I said. After inquiring about several games we both decided checkers would probably be the best for us to play and I guess Ms. Martha approved of that! Quiet frankly, we had a really good time playing checkers, eating cookies, drinking lemonade and just visiting with each other as I know he was probably bored and lonesome. The worst part was I had to keep my shirt and shoes on the whole time I was there.

When time came for me to leave and I do not know who picked the time other than Ms. Martha we shook hands and I told him I had a good time. He told me he had a good time and was wondering if I could come back the next day and before I could answer Ms. Martha spoke from inside the door that I couldn't come back tomorrow because I was going to be busy the next day. The kid was fun to be around and if he could have spent a few hours with Scotty and me he would have had a newer outlook on life. I bet he would have fit right in with us. I always wondered how Ms. Martha thought that I would be busy the next day. I remember while walking home that I had enough cookies in my pockets to keep me busy eating. Old South at its finest. Lemonade, cookies, shoes and shirt! CL

Wendy West adds that the Old South part is that you were obedient to your Mom's will and respectful to your neighbor even though you would have rather been out there doing something else. A rare trait that I have tried to instill in our boys. It has always helped that we had good role models like you boys from Goodwater!

And of course that good role model thing might get rethought after reading the following stories!

Throwing Biscuits

The day Mr. Westbrook got hit in the head with a lunchroom biscuit! At one time the lunchroom workers baked some biscuits that were made from commodity flour and you could play baseball or golf with them. One day a biscuit battle broke out in the lunchroom and a good time was had by all! (You all remember writing thank you notes for English and we ended those practice notes with "and a good time was had by all!") Anyway, the biscuits were a pretty substantial missile! Someone, probably Tommy Dark, threw one all the way across the lunchroom and in the time it was airborne Mr. Westbrook opens the entrance door to the lunch room and was greeted by a biscuit right to his forehead.

He was not happy and the culprit was not going to admit to throwing the biscuit and Mr. Westbrook knew that. Everyone that he thought might be involved was punished by having to wear dress shirts, ties, coat, slacks and shoes fit for church for two weeks.

Well, it did not turn out as he had intended as the young men wore old ties that were eight inches wide, shirts that did not match the tie and slacks and coats that didn't match anything. Immediately Mr. Westbrook knew his mistake but did not say one word. I think the punishment was for two weeks but the young men got to wear their great grandfather's ties. You had to get up way before breakfast to get ahead of a boys mischief in those days. There were no scars but a lot of fun and a lesson taught by Mr. COW. CL

Tommy has this to say about the biscuit throwing. Charlie, I graduated GHS fifty years ago this May. I remember a lot of what all went on back then but this event I don't. I can assure you I never wore any such clothes. If you think hard I bet the guilty party will admit he did it. It was not me. If I had I would admit it! My arm was not that accurate anyway and that's a long way to throw a biscuit. I bet it was someone named Charles!

Sunbathing and Firecrackers!

My best prank on my older sister. It was a hot day and the sun was shining as there was not a cloud in the sky. My sister and one of her girl friends decided that they would work on their sun tan in the back yard. I had been trying to be a part of the company but as you know little brothers were not welcome and I was threatened several times. I was afraid of Sister and even though she was just two years older than me she could beat me up. I felt so lonesome and rejected and had revenge on my mind as they ran me away! They had placed a quilt on a grassy spot and had an extension cord hooked up to our radio and they were tuned in to Rumore's Record Rack and really talking deep secrets.

It was the time when two piece bathing suits had just become popular and they both had one! They were both reclined face down on the quilt with their swim suit top untied and were really tanning. I just wish I could have heard all they were saying. Every time the back door opened Sister would look mean at the door as she thought it was me coming out to pester them. Being the evil genius I was back then I had better thoughts than that. I waited a few minutes and after they had settled down I slipped to the corner of the house that was closest to them. I quietly struck a match and lit a big firecracker (one of those two inch ones) and threw it pretty close to their blanket! BAAAMMMMMMM!

It scared them so bad that they both jumped up and ran into the house as they thought something bad had happened to them. By the way, in their hasty departure they left their swim suit tops on the quilt. I laughed and laughed and ran and ran! I knew I would be in much trouble and I was but it was worth every bit of it. My mama even had to smile at me while she gave me a good scolding. Wish I had one of them phone cameras back then! CL

A Great Birthday Party I will always remember.

I remember my sixth birthday as if it was yesterday. I actually had a party! My mama fixed a chocolate layered cake and Kool-Aid for those coming. I hated that my guest ate most of the cake as it was my favorite kind! The party was on a Saturday at 3:00. My mother required that I take a shower (ugh) at 12:00 so I would be clean for the party and she had prepared my clothes so that I would look nice! I remember that I arranged that Roger Burnett would come at about 2 o'clock so we could play. Roger was a good friend and we were distantly related. He gave me a new baseball for my present! Roger's mother worked with the Cub Scout Pack in Goodwater. I loved my little blue Cub Scout uniform trimmed in a dark yellow or gold!

Anyway, that morning I had been digging a hole about five feet long and about one foot deep. The hole had no purpose other than just digging a hole for the fun of it and I knew I would be made to fill it back up. As we were playing Roger noticed the hole and inquired about it's purpose. I told him I had just dug it for fun. I thought it would be fun if he buried me in it until the other kids arrived and they were wondering where I was. Well, Roger was somewhat reluctant to do that as he was afraid he would get in trouble. I was a lot bigger than Roger so he consented to do as I asked! I placed myself perfectly in the hole for burial! Roger had all of my body covered in dirt with only my head sticking out when my mother came out and observed the situation.

She was so mad and ticked that Roger was scared to death but I thought it was funny. She asked what was going on and I told her I was being buried! She was not pleased and had no problem getting me out of the hole. She did not get on Roger and seemed not to be mad at me.

I did have to take another shower and put on some more clean clothes. Having to shower twice in the same day was bad. I really do not remember much about the party other than I got a new baseball and the other kids ate my cake. I'm sure we all had fun and mama was probably glad when it was over!

One of our games when I was a kid was shooting marbles. I think some were really made out of marble but I believe the "Cat Eyes" were made out of hard clear plastic. They were pretty and most all of a consistent size and they were carried in an old sock as if they were gold. I didn't have many because my mama did not like the idea of me shooting marbles and they cost ten cents for a small bag of about a dozen. That was a two days allowance. I finally saved up a dime and bought a small bag of "Cat Eyes" but I carried them in my pocket. Note! Do not carry marbles in your back pocket if you are subject to getting a paddling as I was! I never carried marbles in my back pocket. I was not that dumb. When I bought my first marbles my mama put down the law. No playing for keeps as that is gambling and if I catch you doing that you will loose all of your marbles!

Now you see what happened was this. I was in Russell School and there were some ole country boys who knew how to shoot marbles but I was not afraid to take them on. The first day I learned a great lesson. If I wanted to keep my marbles I had better not shoot with some of them old boys. I lost all of them before I even got a shot. So, I saved up two more days allowance and bought another bag of marbles. I then played for fun! It was not much fun or macho playing that way as I saw other boys sacks of marbles increase. We and they shot marbles at anytime we were outside and not supervised which was just a few minutes during the day. However, before and after school was another story.

We were usually supervised pretty close as we were subject to fight when we had a difference. Most of the time it was wrestling (rassling) but at times blows were passed. We did not carry guns to school but we all had a jack knife in our pocket but it never occurred to us to cut anyone! However, in high school most boys carried a shot gun in their car during squirrel season as we would go hunting as soon as school was out. Boy, have times changed! Coach James and Gene Hayes had shotguns in their vehicles too. They would go with us at times. And no there were no school shootings back then either! CL

M-80s and the Big Hole

We all have fond memories of this time of year so I thought I would relate an event that happened to myself and my cousin Robert P. Dark. It was Christmas week 1959 . Robert and I were age twelve and being Darks we were always trying something new. He was into making his bicycle look better and I was in to making noise. He took his extra cash and bought things for his bike and I took my cash and bought fireworks.

I had fired off so many black cats back then I was looking to make some more noise. I starting buying all the M-80s I could afford. For those who don't know an M-80 is the equivalent of about a quarter stick of dynamite! I had been buying M-80s from Mr. Rendell Porch for several days that month of December. Not sure exactly how many I had but it was a lot. So off to Roberts house I went on that cold day in December of 1959. We took some 3/4 inch heater hose from his dads shop and Robert and I begin the task of taking the M-80s apart. One end of the hose was taped with duct tape and in went the powder. Not sure how many M-80s we ripped apart that day. I just remember the excitement was building on how it would turn out.

The next thing I remember us doing was packing the powder nice and tight and then taking the fuses from all the M-80s and taping them together. I think we ended up with about three feet of fuse so the good part was about to take place. The total length of the heater hose was probably three foot. We started digging a hole in the ground to bury our new made firecracker and finally we were about to witness something new. Robert, who was actually the mastermind of this, told me to move back and he would strike a match and light the fuse. We both waited from a short distance and then it happened. BOOM would be an understatement!

I think the house they lived in moved at least two feet that day. We both had our faces covered with dirt and pine straw but the mission was accomplished. Of course we had a lot of explaining to do and the best I remember I took the rap and off I went to my friend Tom's house in a hurry. The last time I saw Robert that day he had a shovel in his hand trying to fill in the large hole while I was laughing running through the woods.

Robert said his Mama and Daddy warned him every day not to hang around with me. They said, "That boy just ain't right in the head". Robert also claims to be such a nice young man and felt that I needed a friend that could keep me out of trouble. Well, that didn't work and he found himself more and more involved in my shenanigans.

Just like the firecracker event. It was his fault. I would never think of doing something like that but he was the one who had to fill in the hole. That boy spent his entire youth blaming me for his bright ideas. The following photo Robert claims was taken the day I got out of reform school (the first time)! Actually it was a therapeutic boarding school. I spent three days there and they wanted me to help teach some classes. I told them no because I needed to go home and try and help my cousin Robert.

We kept Kellyton lively for sure and Goodwater in pretty good spirits also. The telephones rang a lot back then warning of our driving habits. I will try and get Robert to tell the one about him leaving the black marks on highway 280 and breaking the axle in the family car. Uncle Bob was never fooled for a minute by his shenanigans. TD

The Chicken

When I was a teenager I enjoyed fun and trying to outsmart people. This incident had me at a stalemate.

In the mid-1960s I worked in a couple of different grocery stores in downtown Goodwater. First I worked at Bob Hammond's Store and later on I worked for Mac Duff Stewart at the Shop Easy Food Store. The incident I am about to tell about happened at Bob Hammond's Store (Formerly W.M. Pruet Store) where I worked in the meat market. As you may remember all meat at that time was sold fresh and not pre-packaged in Canada or Georgia or Lord only knows where! If you bought pork chops, hamburger meat, steak, roast beef or chicken it was cut up that day. We had chickens for sale this particular weekend for $.29/lb. and we sold a lot of them.

As you may remember the stores closed when people quit coming in and that may have been as late as 9:00 pm. It was fairly late this particular Saturday night when a really nice lady came in and wanted to buy a chicken for Sunday dinner and asked me if we had any fryers (young chickens) left. I told her that we did knowing that we had only one chicken left in the stainless steel ice box in the walk-in cooler. I got the normal waxed paper and opened the door to the cooler and reached in and got the last chicken and presented it to her and asked if this one was O.K.? She wanted to know if we had one any larger and I told her I would check.

I took the chicken and shook the ice in the box to indicate I was looking for one larger. Now remember she could not see in the cooler. I presented the same chicken and asked if that one was O.K. and she told me that one was fine. As I was weighing the chicken and preparing to wrap it she made a request that baffled me. She said, "Charles, I believe I will take both of them!" Lordy, Lordy, I can tell you I just had to smile at her and she laughed! I will never forget that as long as I live. What would you have said? CL

What a Summer!

The summer of 1965 was the year I worked my first paying job. I got a job working for the county and commissioner Charlie Buzbee! I seriously thought I would get rich and retire at an early age. There were three of us young men that worked for Coosa County that summer. Our job was to swing a sling blade and cut grass and bushes on the banks where the tractors could not go. We dug fence post holes, strung some barbwire and sometimes got lucky and got to drive the old truck. The other two stooges were Ken Saxon and Charles Luker.

At the end of that summer I received a check for three hundred and fifty dollars. I was able to, with that fortune, buy my first car. Now you understand why I made the statement about what a summer. The car was a 1953 Chevy! I paid three hundred dollars for it and had fifty dollars left over for gas! We didn't worry about insurance in those days! I drove that old Chevy everywhere. The summer of 1966 I traded the 1953 for a 1956. This was a super cool car with a three speed shifter in the floor!

Later on I went to work at Russell Mills and traded for my first new car! A 1967 Chevrolet Camaro SS. I was the king of the road. Y'all have been there. I put about three hundred thousand miles on it before selling it for almost what it cost me new which was $2800. Diane Graham Railey had also bought a new 1967 Camaro. Hers was canary yellow and mine was maroon red. We both were looking good in those Camaros.

I still regret selling all three of those cars! I wish I had them back. Ken has gone on to be with the Lord but Charles and I are still hanging on. So it's my senior year in high school and Charles writes in my year book. He wrote much advice and great words of wisdom and then he wrote, PS 'Remember Pussy'? JL

Tommy writes that would have been the one and only Puss Durden. I also worked for the county the year after the 10th grade and he was our boss. That old mad man worked the heck out of us. Steve Lewis and Gary Shivers were my partners in crime back then. We also pulled a few pranks. Sheriff Mcelrath also worked with us. He tricked me into hitting a wasp nest on county road 40. I got stung so many times my eyes closed together. I did get the rest of the day off though. I never knew their real names but Mr. Buzbee had warned us about P. Durden! TD

Charles adds that Charlie Buzbee and his brother Shine O. Buzbee had a nickname for everyone. My nickname was Joe Palooka. Don't know where it came from but that's what they called me by until the day they died. There was an old fellow that watched after James, Ken and me and Charlie had named him Pussy. The first time I heard it I liked to have fainted. I never called him that to his face but he accepted his nickname and and acted proud to have it as a nickname. He would tell Mr. Buzbee that he cut one side of the road by himself and we couldn't keep up with him. He would cross the road everytime we came to a big field and let us cut it with our swing blades. I know the name sounds off color but it was what it was. Please don't leave anymore like that for me to explain! CL

John Lofton "Charlie" Buzbee, age 99, died Friday December 21, 2007.
Mason "Pussy" Durden, age 76, died May 21, 1974 and is buried at Rehobeth near Nixburg.

Plays, Pageants and Talent Shows

The first play that I recall, mainly because of the pictures that we have, was the Tom Thumb Wedding that our small Goodwater Presbyterian Church sponsored around 1948. The Presbyterians sponsored it so we got most of the best parts. However there weren't enough of us to fill out the whole cast so many others from the Baptist and Methodist churches were recruited to take part.

Linda Robinson was the bride and Bobby Chapman was the groom. Jeanne Ray and I were bridesmaids along with several other girls. Winky Moeling, a groomsman, was my escort. I believe Bobby Sharman was the minister and Betty Sue Chapman was one of the flower girls. Carol Ann Westbrook was also a flower girl if my memory serves. Many others in town had parts playing mothers and fathers of the bride and groom, vocalists and such. It was quite a cast!

The next pageant that I recall was a Christmas pageant in 1949 sponsored by Goodwater Elementary School and included the first and second grades. Today, of course, Christmas pageants in public schools would be strictly prohibited but they were fine sixty-five years ago. I was selected to be Mary. James Gray, whom I have written about earlier in the Halloween street light shooting incident, the bully of the second grade, was slated as Joseph. As a first grader I was terrified of him and did not want to be Mary. I cried about it every night saying I wanted to be an angel like my friends Rose Buttram, Sandra McEwen and Linda Richardson. I begged and begged not to have to be Mary. Finally, one night Mama made me tell her why I was so opposed to being Mary and I said, "Because I'm scared of Joseph!" She convinced me that just because I was Mary did not mean that I had to marry Joseph, so I reluctantly accepted the role with no more tears.

We had lots of talent shows as fund raisers. I had absolutely no talent but I always insisted on singing! This was quite embarrassing for my parents and quite painful for everybody in the audience. Mama would try to convince me to do a tap dance or do a reading or anything besides sing but I would not agree to change my act. We also had countywide 4-H talent shows when we were in high school. Glen Bannister from Rockford, who played piano by ear, was frequently the winner of these. He was really amazing and we all loved to listen to him tear up the piano.

A favorite memory is of my younger cousin Mike Smith singing "There's No Business Like Show Business" in one of the talent shows when he was about seven years old. He was small and very cute and began, like Al Jolson, singing the opening line "There's no business like show business" to the top of his lungs. He was stooping over and throwing both arms out to his sides like a real showman. The problem was he could not remember the next line. He would then start over, from the top, with the big opening and then stop again. This went on for about four or five times with the audience getting more and more amused. Finally somebody in a rather loud 'stage whisper' gave him the second line so he could go on and finish the song.

Around 1954 or 1955 we had a May Day pageant and I got to be The May Queen. This was probably because I was taking dance lessons from Miss Marie in Alex City. Also whoever was in charge of the pageant figured that they could get my Mama to design a pretty coronation robe for me to wear! Each class at Goodwater Elementary School participated and the pageant was held on the football field. After each class did their dance they would then stand in front of the May Day Court and bow. Mike Swindall declared that he had no intention of bowing to me! I expect his mama told him that he would do whatever Mrs. Evans told him to do so he complied but with a twist. Since his back was turned to the audience when he bowed he stuck out his tongue at the same time! He also encouraged all of the others to do the same so that only the court saw this flagrant gesture of disrespect from our not-so-humble subjects!

Mrs. Evans, who only worked part-time at Goodwater Elementary and High Schools, was quite talented in putting on skits and plays with the little bit of talent that she had to work with. We managed to get cute and colorful home-made costumes for the various musical productions. I believe it was a tradition for a while for each Senior Class to put on a play and I can remember one class doing a remarkably good production of "Huckleberry Finn". That may have been the class that Neal Westbrook was in. Just like his daddy he had a good voice and I think he had the leading role.

By the time I was a senior in 1960-61, we no longer put on a class play. As I recall, we did have a class night where the seniors did various things. I don't remember too much about how this was organized but we were all involved in some way. The good thing about the various kinds of productions that we had was that generally everybody was involved and got some experience in being on stage. BDB

Tom Thumb wedding. Photo Courtesy Pamela Kellogg

Clyde and Kate

Well this is not really a story it was just the way Clyde was. Clyde owned a pretty good bird dog named "Kate." Clyde loved that dog but would talk ugly to Kate but Kate didn't know what Clyde was saying other than his tone of voice changed and Kate would shy down. I had a bird dog that Clyde had given me and I named him "Clyde." The dog was really smart and liked to bird hunt and like to find the coveys. I carried Clyde, Kate and "Clyde" hunting several times and it was a rather interesting experience.

Once Clyde left the truck his shotgun was ready to fire at all times. He never had the safety on. It was a good practice to hunt at least fifty yards away from Clyde as he was subject to stumble around a good bit. I remember late one afternoon we were hunting the Chapman Cemetery cut-over and the dogs were smelling birds and were really cutting off area by area to try to point the birds. All at once Clyde fired his shotgun and I looked at where he was and he was just stumbling around like nothing had happened. Lordy, his gun had went off. I ask him if he had killed the bird and his response was not one typical of a choir boy!

Once, we were hunting and the dogs had started smelling birds and we had to go through a thick pine thicket. I could tell the birds were running and I told Clyde for us not to rush the dogs and let's stop and rest a minute and he agreed. He needed another mouth full of snuff anyway I guess. I told him I would hold his gun while he got a dip and he handed me his shotgun and I clicked his safety on!! A few minutes later Kate's bell had quit jingling and I could see that "Clyde" was backing Kate up and we eased in to flush the covey that had been pointed in a little open field. When the birds flushed I think I got two and Clyde was over their just cussing about someone messing with his shotgun as it wouldn't shoot. I pointed out that he had accidentally had the guns safety on and it wouldn't shoot. We were hunting single birds for a few minutes with Clyde shooting at two or three but I stayed way behind him. Gladly, we went home after that! Clyde loved Kate so much that he let her sleep with him in his bed! Poor Kate! CL

Car AC

I am thinking that we were the first family in Goodwater to own a station wagon. My father bought it from Wilbanks Motors in Alex City. When Goodwater decided to go to parallel parking spaces they had to use our car to measure them off because of its size!!

That car was really ahead of its time! It held all of us for our trips to Florida and it held all our suitcases too! Not only that but it had a new gadget too, air conditioning! Mother was at Lynna's beauty shop one Saturday morning and she was telling all in hearing about how nice it was to be so cool and comfortable while travelling. A friend of hers, Faye Smith, wanted to check it out so out to the car they went. They got in, rolled up the windows and mother turned on the air and waited on that cool air to provide some relief from the oppressive heat. After about ten minutes and three gallons of sweat and droopy hair, Faye decided air conditioning in a car might not be all it was cracked up to be! They both got out and went back inside! Mother had no idea why it didn't work as usual until she got home and related the tale to my dad. He, snickering under his breath, told her she had to start the car so it would cool! Celia Burns

Papa Jim and the Possum

Long before having a television or attending movies with modern day heroes like John Wayne or Randolph Scott I had a hero. His name was 'Papa Jim'. He was my grandfather, James Dowdwell Dark, who was born in 1881. He lived in a very small house about 300 yards from our house. I had the privilege of knowing him until he left us for a better place in 1965.

He taught me how to sharpen a knife and use it in a safe manner. We built forts in the woods from pine saplings. He would share stories from his boyhood that just kept me spellbound. When I had the opportunity to spend the night at his house he would read to me from the Bible. He would then explain what he had just read and relate it into modern times so that I could better understand it. I loved him dearly.

When I was a wee lad of around five or so Papa-Jim and I were on one of our adventures in the woods and ran across a sulled-up 'possum on the ground. That thing was making a hissing sound and had his lips rolled back to show us his needle sharp teeth. That was simply his defense mechanism. Papa Jim eased up to that old 'possum and very carefully grabbed him behind the neck with one hand and with the other grabbed his tail. He picked that 'possum up and turned to me and said, "That's how we used to catch them when I was a young man". Then he let the old 'possum go on its way. Boy, was I impressed!

A few months later I was meandering through the woods alone and ran across a big old fat sulled-up 'possum. Remembering how Papa Jim had executed the capture I put my knowledge into action and caught that big rascal. I couldn't wait to show Papa Jim my prize. I headed off toward Papa Jim's house with that fat-boy around the neck with one hand and had his old rat-like tail in the other. I walked into Papa Jim's door clinging for dear life to that old 'possum and announced, "Papa Jim, look what I caught". Papa Jim came from the other room and began hollerin' at me to get back outside. "I mean, get outside now!" I was devastated! Why did he not appreciate my trophy?

I went outside and Papa Jim followed me. Once outside he said "Let that thing go now and look at your clothes". It seems that on the trip through the woods to Papa Jim's house that ole fat boy had relieved himself of all those poke berries and whatever else he had been eating.

The front of my new denim jacket and my jeans were covered in a purple looking sludge. I was covered from my chest to my shoes with "possum crap"!

I had to make my way back up the hill to my house and explain to Mama how I came to be in such a terrible state. Mama was not a happy camper! However after stripping me down and throwing those clothes in the old wringer washer everything was once again copacetic. (Look it up, it's a word that Papa Jim taught me).

That pretty much ended my 'possum catching days. I have attached a photo of the actual 'possum catching' outfit that I wore that day. Long live "Papa Jim" and his memories which influenced my life in those days and still do today. RD

The Comet

My cousin Robert and I were just young boys trying to figure out what the world was all about. We both joined the United States Air Force when we were eighteen so it didn't take long for us to sure enough discover how things were in the world. My dad's car, a 1956 Ford, was mine for the using until I got grounded so many times that he took it away from me.

These were family cars. A way back then a family of four normally had only one vehicle and in some cases the father had a truck. No way were we going to get to drive the fathers truck so the family car was our only option. We had to ask in advance if we could use it. In my family my dad would always inspect it the next day after I used it for things like beer cans and such. If one was found then that was the end of the car for me.

The school parking lot had very few vehicles in it when I was in school. Thanks to my brother who liked to buy and sell I soon had me a ride and I was back in business. I still had to go by the rules even though the car was mine. I had many cars tied to the old oak tree close to our house because I just could not go by the so called Dark rules Never any trial was held, I was just always found guilty. Many of the times it would be my cousin Roberts fault but they nailed me!

One incident I remember occurred at the Kellyton Methodist Church. It went something like this. Robert and I had went for a ride between Sunday School and the 11:00 am church service. We both liked to smoke back then. We rode to my dads shop and had our break lighting up. On the way back I told him to make sure all the cigs were out of the car. One of us and I have always thought it was him tossed the smoke out the front window just before we turned into the church parking lot. We went in for the 11:00 am service.

When we came out around noon there was smoke coming from the back seat area of my car. There was nothing left of the rear seat except the springs. Then all the blame started. Of course nobody knew who did it but I knew that it was not me because it was my car and I sure paid attention to the cigarette when I threw it out. Now I doubt you will ever get a confession from Robert. He blamed it on some of the old men who were smoking in the parking area but that did not happen. Who did it? I do not have a clue. I am 100% sure it was not me because I always looked when I tossed one out.

Of course it was in the summer and all the windows were down so who knows what happened. All I know is I had to find a new (used) rear seat for my car and never could get the smell out. I finally sold the car and bought another one!

In early 1965 I was thinking about how I could talk my dad into a new car. I told him, well you bought my brother a new car in 1961 so it would be only fair if you did the same for me. At first he said no but I kept on it until he gave in under one condition. I had to pay extra money because cars had went up in price since 1961. Of course I was quick to agree to pay him $25 per month and I got a new 1965 Comet. I was now in business for sure. I continued to drive this Comet and find ways to make it go faster without Pop knowing about it. I also kept getting caught by him and I had to remove what I had added to it.

I drove this car until I left for the Air Force the next year. It sit idle waiting on me to return for a thirty day leave. I came home in January of 1968 and I had so much missed the Comet. While out riding one night soon after I came home on leave I tried to outsmart the law one more time. This time things did not work like in the past and I ended up in a creek with my nice clean Comet wrecked beyond repair.

My dad was not at all pleased with me and he said he was just taking what was left of my car and I could find a way to go the best I could. I just left and went back to Ramey AFB and never came back until I could buy me a new 1970 Road Runner.

As Robert said Kellyton was never the same after we both left in 1966. Things were again nice and quite and very little hot rodding took place. The Comet with my brother Charles. TD

Churches

There were three main churches I remember growing up in Goodwater. I'm glad that we had them since I regularly attended all three as a child. As Presbyterians we only had Sunday services twice a month since our pastor also served the Hatchet Creek and Socapatoy churches as well. Consequently, we would go to the Baptist Church for services once a month and to the Methodist Church the other Sunday after attending Sunday School at our little church. When I decided to join the church I announced to Mama that I planned to join all three! She said that I couldn't do that and I replied that I didn't see why not since I went to all of them. She said I needed to wait a little longer until I could decide on just one.

I also joined the various youth groups at the other churches as well. I was in the Rosebud choir at one, a member of Sunbeams at another, whatever there was to join that my friends were in. I showed up in those as well. My daddy died on a Sunday night in September of 1957, shortly before I turned fourteen. That Sunday we had gone to the Presbyterian church for Sunday School, to the Methodist church for the 11:00 service and to the Baptist church for the Sunday night service. We figured that was a pretty good way for somebody to have spent his last day on earth! I appreciate all the sweet people in all of the churches who made us feel so welcome. BDB

Lee Swindall West says she was the same way. I went to Girls in Action (GA's) at the Baptist Church although I grew up at Goodwater Presbyterian. The Methodist parsonage was just behind our house so we were good friends with the Havens when he was the Methodist minister. Our church had burned and had not been rebuilt when Doug and I got married. So we were married in the Baptist Church by Brother Havens.

Nancy Nail Carter relates a wonderful memory in her little white church!! I remember when our piano teacher, Mrs Dorothy Robbins, would assign us students different Sunday nights to play the hymns at evening worship! I would practice and practice! Sometimes I would go to the church and practice while my older brother Jimmy cleaned the church! I believe he and Charlie Luker did it together! Anyway while I (we) played on Sunday nights our friends were in the congregation and sometimes we all got tickled! Sometimes the hymnal would fall and we'd lose our place. But everyone kept singing. They were so nice to put up with us!

The Bologna Sandwich

I was about ten or so and out and about on my bicycle and stopped at one of the local stores. I only had a nickle so all I could buy was a soft drink if I didn't leave with the bottle. That would require a deposit and I was a bit shy on funds. Not like I was going anywhere anyway! There was a meat cooler and one of the things the man kept in there was a log of bologna. When I say log that is exactly what I mean. This thing was about six inches wide and three feet long. At least! You would order a pound or whatever and he would cut it off, weight it and wrap it for you in wax paper.

These two guys were there also and it was about noon or so. They had just went in and ordered a pound of bologna, a loaf of bread and a small jar of mustard. Mustard only came in glass jars at that time and they got the smallest one. Then they went outside under the carport area of the store and sat on some wooden soda crates and started their repast. Set up a few crates to make a table.

The first order of business was to remove the rind on the bologna. This was some kinda red plastic wrapper or something that is pretty much not used nowadays. Usually this would pull off cleanly but occasionally it would pull off bits of the bologna. The proper protocol in this instance was to pull the film between your teeth to strip off the little pieces of meat. Then they started cutting off slabs of bologna with their pocket knives. Now these knives were what they used to clean their fingernails, skin squirrels and other unspeakable things with the only cleaning being a good swipe on a dirty, sweaty pant leg! Plus the Lord only knew when they had washed their hands last! Then the knife was uses to slather the bread with a good helping of the mustard. This was all then put together and the feast was at hand. That and a sixteen ounce Nehi orange drink and you had a meal.

Well I hadn't ate since breakfast but could usually scrounge up something when I was out and about. If you were at a friends house at meal time you were invariably invited to share. I had had no such luck on this day and all I had was the nickle and glad to have it so that I could at least get a soft drink. So I asked one of the men if I could have a bit of the bologna and just one slice of bread. Being a good Christian he readily said yes and to my surprise cut off a slab about a quarter inch thick and dressed two slices of bread with the mustard and handed the sandwich to me. I went and got a Grapico and sat with them and ate.

Some of you are probably wondering where the hoop cheese was. Well, it was on the counter in the store but they hadn't bought any as I guess they were a bit shy on funds too. A lot of that going around back then! Now I consider myself somewhat of a connoisseur of bologna and have had it in all manner of ways. I've had fried bologna, barbequed bologna, sweet and sour bologna, bologna tacos, bologna gravy with eggs, etc. but looking back on it I believe that was the best bologna sandwich I ever had! PGG

Clyde and the Buzzard

Clyde was not much of a traveller as he had a limited means of travel other than walking. He did go to other parts of the county to help, train or maybe learn how to make 'shine. He told me of one of his journeys to west Coosa County to help a good friend make a run of 'shine. I won't use the man's name as he later became a good friend of mine. He really had a deep trust for me and I always enjoyed stopping by to see him. That was pretty unusual in itself because he only had a limited list of friends that he trusted.

Clyde and this man (we'll call Bart) had been at the still all night running the shine off and both were black from the pine knots and logs that they had been using to heat the pot with. They were also tired from the nights work and both were hungry. Upon entering where Bart lived they both could smell a roasting hen or turkey in the old stove. They both got around the kitchen table to prepare for some of the roasting delicacy. Bart opened the stove and was delighted to see a big hen fully roasted and ready for consumption. Bart got both a plate and they pulled part of the roasted hen off and started to eat. Only a few moments had passed and they were engrossed in eating the roasted delight when Bart's mama walked in and rather loudly got on to the both of them as she let them know that they were eating her buzzard that she had baked for the grease! The buzzard grease was an old folk remedy for salve to use on her arthritis! Clyde had a hard time telling this as he was laughing and had a mouth full of snuff and was quivering so much. Clyde had Parkinson's Disease in his later years but it didn't hinder his bird hunting. CL

Mr. Clifford Holman and his family lived not too far from Clyde. Late one evening Clyde walked up to Mr. Holman's house and had three or four old dogs following him. A thunder shower came up and Mr. Holman offered to drive Clyde (and his dogs) home. About the time they loaded those dogs into the back seat of Mr. Holman's old car Mrs. Holman came out and told Clyde that supper was ready and she would be glad to have him eat with them.

After supper they went back out to the car in order to make the trip to Clyde's house. When they opened the doors of that car the dogs had ripped up the seat covers and door panels so bad that all you saw was strips of vinyl, seat padding and springs. They even tore the head-liner out of the ceiling. Mr. Holman took Clyde and the dogs on home anyway and he just chalked it up to experience. RD

Papa Jim and checking on the Neighbors

I have mentioned elsewhere that my Grandfather, Papa Jim, was born in 1881. He was raised as most of his kids were on a farm in a small community called Keno located in Coosa County. By the time I was old enough to remember him his farming days were over and he lived in a small house about three hundred yards from where I was raised in Kellyton. One of the things that I remember about him was that every morning just shortly after day break, I would hear him 'holler'. Then late in the evening just before sundown, I would hear him holler again. I could hear him even if I was inside the house. It was loud. His morning holler was different than his evening holler.

I asked him one time why he did this twice each day. He told me that it was the way neighbors communicated in the olden days. Your closest neighbor may be a half mile or more away and there were no telephones and most didn't even have electricity. How did the world ever survive without cell phones? Life was very simple, but effective in those days. So every morning one neighbor would yell something like "oooooo-weeeeeeee". Then the other neighbors within earshot would answer with their own distinct call. Every neighbor knew the other neighbor's call. That first call and answer session let everyone know that all was well. This was repeated just before dark with another distinct call and answer. This let the neighbors know that the work day was over and everything was fine.

He said that if a neighbor was in trouble then yet another call was used. These calls could be heard by surrounding farmers as there was no noise from tractors or other motorized vehicles. Only farm sounds which sometimes included the sound of the old plow mule breaking wind. He continued those calls as long as I can remember. The times had changed for him and the only person that ever answered his calls late in his life was me. The next time my cell phone rings I may just answer it, "oooooooo-weeeeee", then hang up. RD

Bethy Trout says her Daddy could verify this story as he used to tell us Papa Jim's voice would carry further than anyones. Dad said he and his brothers would be working far down in the fields in the land of Keno. Papa Jim would be squatted on a stump up near the house hollerin' at them, giving directions, corrections and assorted salutations!

Chained to the Tree Again!

When I was age sixteen the only way I knew how to drive a car was wide open as I just had a need for speed. My routine was always the same. I got out of Goodwater High School and drove home quickly to get ready to work in my dad's shop. This one day I had got home from school, ate a quick snack and off to the shop I went.

Just as I started to drive off I noticed my dad's truck heading my way. I stopped to see what he was doing coming home at this time of day. However in the drivers seat was my cousin Bill Dark and no Pop as far as I could see. I chatted with Bill for a few seconds and told him I needed to get to work.

When I took off I thought maybe I would show Bill my superior driving skills so I put the pedal to the metal. I took off fishtailing all the way down that old dirt driveway almost wrecking several times. The dust was flying probably some two hundred feet in the air. I slowed for only a second prior to entering the blacktop highway. As I hit the pavement on the old Kellyton road I did what many of us young people did back then, I burned rubber, lots of it! I looked back and marvelled at how long a black mark I had left. It was indeed a beauty. I plotted that if I was ever asked about who made the tire marks I planned to blame it on my cousin Robert!

I drove into the parking lot of the shop, jumped out and asked my brother Charles what he had for me to do. He said to get the broom and sweep the floor until he found me something to do. I then asked where Pop was. He said, "Oh, him and Bill went to the house to look for some old tractor parts that was stored in one of the barns."

Then it hit me! Where was my dad when I did the burn out? I didn't see him in the truck so where was he?! I also begin to worry that maybe he had witnessed my crazy ways and I was in big trouble.

After about fifteen minutes or so had passed here comes Pop's old Ford truck but this time he was driving. He walked over to me and asked for the keys to my car. There was no need to argue. I was in big trouble so I just tossed them to him! Bill had a funny smile on his face that I can still see in my mind till today. My dad had been hiding down low in the truck all the time I was chatting to Bill that day. Pop told Charles to follow him to the house and my car was again chained to the old oak tree.

I still wonder why Bill did not tip me off that day? He could have rolled his eyes toward the floorboard or something! Guess he was in on the joke. My wayward cousin Robert probably put them up to it knowing I was planning on blaming him for the tire marks!

I had to sneak out the back door for two weeks in order to continue to go out on the weekends. Obviously I couldn't go in the chained up car. I finally got it back but not for long as my speedy ways continued. I finally left home at age eighteen for service with my Uncle Sam never to return. What a mess I was back then but I think I turned out pretty good in life despite all my crazy ways in my youth. TD

Hamlet

Several months ago an old friend of mine came by the Courthouse to visit. He is a retired literature professor from The University of North Alabama and naturally he wanted to talk literature. I informed him that I had to take one course in literature to graduate and was glad to get out of it with a passing grade. I told him that the only part of literature I liked was Shakespeare's "Hamlet".

As we were talking about Hamlet a county commissioner who shall remain nameless walked in and wanted to know what we were talking about. I introduced the two and told the commissioner that we were talking about Hamlet or rather the tragedies of Hamlet. I ask him if he knew anything about Hamlet. He informed me that he did and as a matter-of-fact he had one last week at the Huddle House! With toast and coffee! Gotta love life in a small town!CL

Hilltop and Recess

In the 1950s there was no P.E. class at Goodwater Elementary School on The Hilltop. We were taken outside and told to play with very little supervision. I recall the girls in our class bringing colored pieces of broken glass to school and we would get together in a group and try to make things with the beautiful fragments. The boys took great pleasure in pestering us and in running through our little circle and messing up our creations! One day we had had enough and decided that we would retaliate.

We collected some rocks to throw at the boys when they stampeded through our artistic endeavors. I must have gotten a fairly good sized rock and threw it at Winky Moeling and hit him very close to his eye. He had to be taken to the doctor and had to get two or three stitches to close the wound. Of course, I was scared and didn't really mean to hurt Winky. When my Mama found out that I had been the one to throw the rock she was horrified. She made me call Winky and apologize. We learned that if the rock had landed just a fraction closer to his eye it could have blinded him. He still has a tiny scar right next to his eye as a reminder of that day at recess.

Another day at recess I was the victim. We had a piece of playground equipment that we called a merry-go-round. It was circular with a wooden bottom and had some steel dividers that we would hold onto. We would hold on to the steel handles and run to make it go fast and then we would all jump on and ride. Then when it slowed down we would all jump off and run around some more, etc. There were so many of us jumping on and jumping off that it was a wonder that more accidents didn't occur. You could have easily gotten trampled if you didn't keep up. This one day I was somehow knocked off of it and my left leg got caught underneath. There were huge bolts that secured the wooden floor to the steel handles and those bolts kept tearing away at my knee. Finally when everybody realized what was going on I believe Rose Buttram helped hold it up somehow so that it wouldn't continue to cut into my leg. Soon some teachers came over and helped get it all under control. I had a very ugly looking wound! The muscles and tendons in my knee were bulging out from the nasty wound. I wound up having to have several stitches in my leg and a tetanus shot. I still have an ugly scar on my knee as a reminder of that incident.

It's a wonder that more bad accidents did not happen since our recess/play time was so loosely organized and supervised. However back then the teachers didn't have a break all day long except for recess, so they usually just sat together and talked while we roamed all over the playground inventing games of our own. BDB

Charles says this story brought back the following memory. Betty mentioned broken pieces of colored glass and that reminded me of two games that my sister, Martha Jean and I played for hours. The game that we enjoyed most was hop-scotch! We would get in the yard and with a stick draw our hop-scotch court. Then we would use different pieces of colored glass as our toy or throwing piece and the game was on. As all of you may know you began by tossing your toy into the first square and then had to hop one-legged over that first square and then all the way to the end of the court. There you would turn around with a hop and come back to the beginning still having to hop over your own toy. As long as you didn't miss a square with your toss of your toy, make a miss hop or have to put both feet down you continued advancing up the court until you missed. When you missed you left your toy in the last square that you had successfully finished and then your opponent had their turn. Then when your opponent advanced on the court they had to hop over that square each time. It got interesting and usually ended with an argument about landing on a line either by your foot or your toy!

The second activity was less complicated! Jump Sticks! This was a running long jump as seen in track meets absent the sand box to land in. Martha and I could both jump a long way and had heated competition. My greatest jump occurred as Martha and I were competing in our front yard in a little flat area that was shaded by a big oak tree. Here we had to start our sprint and cross the sidewalk at great speeds before we jumped. I don't know what happened but on the jump I felt as if I were flying! I fell forward on my landing and hit on my stomach with my left hand in front of me. I knew when I landed something was not right by the severe pain in my wrist. I cried!!!

Martha Jean just laughed until she realized I was really hurt. Papa carried me to see Dr. H.L. Cockerham and he took an X-ray and in a few minutes informed me that I had fractured my lower arm. (I believe the ulna). He applied a cast that I was told to wear for six weeks. Boy, I thought I wouldn't have to take a bath for six weeks! I was wrong again! Yes it itched a little but not near as bad as the cast I had on my leg in later years. The bad part is it was early spring and my baseball playing was delayed by several weeks. All part of growing up I guess. As all of you have done as kids we ran and jumped all of the time. We ran everywhere we went. And threw rocks which were our number one weapon! CL

Best Nap Ever

It was the summer of 1961. I was soon to turn fifteen years of age. My Dad's oldest brother, Uncle Sam, offered me a job paying $5.00 per week feeding his cows every afternoon. I jumped at the opportunity because it meant that I got to drive his WWII surplus Army Jeep. All I had to do was to load bales of hay in the back of the jeep, drive around to a couple of different places in his pasture, cut the twine holding the bales together and let the cows have their fill. I always had to make two trips from the newly built barn where the hay was stored. The jeep only held so many bales and he had quite a few cows.

One hot summer day I was making the second trip to the barn to refill the hay in the jeep and a typical Alabama summertime thunder shower came out of nowhere. I pulled the jeep into the all-tin barn to wait until the shower passed. For some reason, I decided to lay across a stack of baled hay and enjoy the sounds of the raindrops pounding on the tin roof. The fresh smell of a summer rain, the sudden coolness of the atmosphere and the amplified sound of raindrops hitting that roof was just too much for me. I fell asleep! I don't remember how long I slept, but when I awoke, I had a feeling like none before and none since. I was so refreshed. I wanted that feeling to last forever.

I am gaining on sixty-eight years in age and I have not had that feeling since. I have never been able take a nap in the afternoon as I always awake groggy and feel like a UPS delivery truck just ran me over. Not only do I feel bad after a nap but I usually wind up staring at the ceiling fan all night long. I think quite a bit about that rainy summer afternoon when I was just fourteen years old. I don't think I will ever be able to have such a refreshing and peaceful feeling again. Apparently, some things in our short journey through life are meant to be experienced only once. Not long after that wonderful adventure I lost my job feeding the cows. I decided to invite my cousin Tommy Dark and long-time friend, Gary Shivers to help me feed the cows. We did more Jeep-riding than cow-feeding but that's another story. RD

The Big Bam Show, Lou Christie and the Holstein Cow.

By the time of my senior year most of the gang had an old car that they drove everywhere. On special occasions any one of us might borrow the family car. The Big Bam show was coming to Montgomery and some of us boys had ordered tickets. We would quite often go out of town to Birmingham, Montgomery and sometimes to Panama City. Charles Luker had borrowed his family car for the trip to see Lou Christie at the Big Bam show. We had a wonderful time and Lou brought the house down with "Lightnin' Strikes" I remember a lot of the old folks trying to get the song banned as being too vulgar. One man I remember saying, "If that song stays on the air there will be teenagers having sex behind every tree." I began to look behind trees but never saw anyone doing anything!

Charles, Eddie Dickerson, Tommy Nail, Johnny Turner, Bobby Mann, Wally Bridges and myself loaded up to go to the show. I'm not sure if this list is correct but we were always together. There were no drugs or alcohol involved on the night just a good and fun time together. On the way back to Goodwater we were on highway nine almost to Equality and Charles is driving the speed limit or just over. Suddenly there appeared in front of us a huge Holstein cow! There was no way to miss her, we are about to crash and someone yells, "Help us Jesus!" I still believe that cows can fly!

I love the Chick-Fil-A commercials with the cows on the roof tops so cows must fly. Only by the grace of God did Charles miss that cow or maybe it did sprout wings and fly just a few feet so a car of young men might return home safely. We began to call Charles by the last name of Petty. Charles and I talked about that night in 1966 not too long ago. We both are in agreement that it was only God's Grace that saved us. It saved us that night and it has also saved us for eternity. Joshua 1:5 Just as I was with Moses, so I will be with you. I will not leave you or forsake you. God Bless. JL

The Persimmon

My Grandma Rogers lived her last few years in Brown's Nursing Home and my sister Martha Jean and I went to school in Alex City where mama taught school. I always had to sit in the back seat going to and from school as sister had to sit in the front and control the radio listening to all of those old songs on Rumore's Record Rack or some other station such as The Big Bam. I even enjoyed the news at that time but it might have been because MJ wanted to listen to those old songs!

After school we would always stop so we would go in to see Grandma. Mama would sometimes let us stay in the car. I really don't remember if this incident happened after school in late spring or after we had been swimming during the summer. Anyway, there was a big persimmon tree close to where we always parked when we visited Grandma and on this particular day mama let us stay in the car. I knew what a persimmon looked like and I knew MJ didn't so I got out and acted as if I was eating a crab apple but of course I knew better! I got back in the car and told MJ that was the best crab apple that I had ever eaten. It was so juicy and bitter that it made my hair stand up I told her. I also told her that I would be glad to get her one off of the tree if she would eat it and she said she wanted one. I got her one and got in the back seat and she chomped down on that persimmon and took half of it in one bite. I started laughing as soon as she had taken the bite and she chewed that thing and turned around and threw it at me! She hit me and it hurt but I was laughing so hard I thought her next move was to kill me. Anyway, she couldn't talk and her mouth was puckered up and she was really telling me some stuff.

When mama returned MJ told her about how I had tricked her and how she was going to beat me up when we got home and she could too. By the time we had travelled the fourteen miles home she had lost her pucker and was in a better humor! I felt that was equal payback for having to listen to her music for several years. Mama scolded me when we got home but she was smiling. After that I would never eat or drink anything MJ fixed for me. I guess her payback was when I cracked and picked out a bunch of pecans for a German Chocolate Cake. I would pick out two cups of pecans and she and big sister would roast and eat one cup! Mean to the bone!
CL

Snake in the Creek

One hot summer many years ago my boyhood friend Bobby and his cousin Buddy who was visiting from California decided we needed to go cool off. This meant going to the creek. Now there were several creeks in the area so we decided to go to Mathis Creek. This is not "The Official" name but it's what we called it. It was near where my Aunt Mary Ellen lived but that's another story. You could actually drive pretty close to the area where we would go swimming. There used to be a field there where corn or cotton or some such was grown years ago but it had gone into disuse over the years and now only grew sage brush. Sage brush could be harvested and bundled and tied to a stick to make a primitive broom which we did on occasion and used to brush the yard out front of Grannie's house to get rid of the leaves, walnut husks and such so we could draw 'roads' in the dirt to play with our stick cars and trucks. I believe my sister from Hell used said broom to ride on but I have no photographic proof! Used to hear shrieks in the middle of the night and she was nowhere to be found! Got a little side tracked there!

Anyway there was this 'road' on the side of the field that was furthest from the creek. So we drive out there and park. I was about fourteen at the time but had been driving for about two years or so. Bobby and Buddy were about a year younger. We go through the field to this area where we know there is a big bank on one side, gentle slope on the other and a nice curve in the creek right before it gets to the deep part where we went swimming. The bank was an important part of this arrangement as you could run and leap off the bank and fly about ten-twelve feet before you hit the water. Poor boy diving board if you will! Well, being poor we did not have bathing suits and as we were about a quarter mile from the road which wasn't well traveled anyway we did what most boys our age did. Skinny dipping! Plus the banks were pretty well overgrown with bushes and such. You could have hid WMD's there with no problem. We had dug hand holes in the red clay of the bank so we could climb out of the creek to leap again. These would get real slippery and such as they got wet and you had to be careful.

So there we are swimming and jumping and all of a sudden coming around the bend where the curve in the creek was comes this snake just floating down the water. Not sure what kind of snake. Didn't know if it was a water moccasin, water snake or the dreaded and deadly copper-headed water rattler!

Now this caused some consternation among the ones in the creek as you can imagine. We started yelling, "Snake! Snake!" The one that was really surprised was Buddy as he had just jumped off the bank and was headed for a direct hit on the snake who was just casually floating down the creek without a care in the world. Now I know you have seen cartoons where the character stops in midair and changes direction. We both know that this is impossible but I saw it happen that day! In the meantime Bobby and myself are trying to get up the bank using the hand holds we dug that are designed for one person but now there are two people trying to occupy the same space at the same time. That old Alabama red clay is wet and it is as slick as owl snot. Grasping and fighting and slipping and sliding! Naked! Trying not to touch each other. Plus all the screaming, splashing and carrying on going on behind us and that was just the snake! Don't believe we ever went swimming there again! PGG

Clyde the XXX-rated One

One morning during the late spring my wife, Melinda, came in the Tax Office to see me and I could tell she was a bit "flustered" as she had witnessed something not known to her normal routine. She questioned me about something she had seen that morning as she was pulling out of our drive. I guessed a big deer and the answer was NO! I guessed a wild turkey and the answer was again NO! I guessed a spaceship landing in our pasture and the answer was NOOOO!

I politely told her I didn't have any idea what she saw and would she please reveal what she had seen. She asked if I wanted one more guess and I told her that I did not and I had some things I needed to do. OK she replied! I saw Clyde standing on his front porch this morning "NEKKID!" To add some excitement I asked if he had any shoes on and she again said he was completely NEKKID!

She had turned red in the face with embarrassment and I calmly told her that it was alright that that was just Clyde's early morning call to nature but I sternly asked her if she looked a second time. She confessed that she had as she wasn't real sure that what she was seeing was real! I sadly told her that the first look was not a sin but the sin was committed when she looked the second time! She left laughing. I wonder if she looked ever morning after that sighting!

Imagine, if you can, just glancing over and unexpectedly seeing an eighty-five year old man nekkid on his front porch. CL

Clyde's Wallet

I've got to tell this one on Clyde! One morning as I was leaving home for work I had to pass by Clyde's house and there he was sitting on his front porch eating watermelon with Artis Whetstone. When I passed by I knew something was wrong as they were sitting on opposite sides of the porch and both looking down! Immediately I backed up and I asked Artis what in the world was wrong. First let me say that Mr. Artis Whetstone is probably one of the finest men I have ever known! Honest, humble and would help anyone in need! Artis told me that Clyde had said someone had stolen his billfold and thought that Artis had done it! Well, knowing Artis,I knew that was not so.

Clyde wore overalls and kept his wallet in the top zippered pocket along with his snuff. Clyde had indoor plumbing but never adapted to it.

He chose the bushes for his calls to nature and in more particular a grape vine just below his house! I ask Clyde if he had been to the grapevine this morning and he indicated he had and I told them that was probably where his wallet was! Sure enough I followed both of them to the vicinity of the grape vine and heard Artis holler "Praise the Lord Mr. Charlie there it is!" I knew that when Clyde had dropped his overalls the wallet had fell out!

They then went back to the front porch and were sitting on the same side of the porch eating their watermelon as I left! At seven am! Clyde never said thank you or apologized! His apology was moving his watermelon half to the same side of the porch as Artis. Actions sometimes speak louder than words! CL

What's left of Clyde's old front porch.

Water Wells, Dynamite and Toting Water

My Daddy built a small house on a hill in Kellyton somewhere around 1948. At some point he hired a couple of fellows to dig a well. They went down about twelve feet and hit solid granite. Through much effort they managed to go on down to about thirty feet and actually struck some water. That water was filtered through that blue granite and it was the best tasting water I have ever put in my mouth. The only problem was the well would go dry in the fall of the year and we would have to tote water. We usually got water from Mr. Zoland Waites one of our church members. This lasted from about October through February as we simply had no well water.

Somewhere along about 1960 or so, Daddy hired a well drilling outfit out of Sylacauga to drill us a new well. They sank a two hundred foot deep shaft right next to the drilled well and only got dry blue granite powder. Over the next couple of years he had another drilled about forty yards away. Again dry powder! Then he drilled another about sixty yards in the other direction. Well, you guessed it, dry powder! This went on until a total of six wells had been drilled around that hill and nothing but dry powder came from them. We always went back to the original hand dug well.

One of the one hundred foot deep drilled wells showed some promise with just a little water seepage and someone suggested that if we could somehow set off an explosion in the bottom of that well then we might just jar a vein of water loose and the well would produce. Back in those days you could buy dynamite at the local hardware store. My Daddy bought eight sticks and a couple of blasting caps from Robinson Hardware in Goodwater. He also bought five gallons of diesel fuel and a couple of bags of Nitrate of Soda fertilizer.

Now those drilled wells were usually only about six to eight inches in diameter and they would drive a twenty foot long piece of steel pipe into the drilled hole in order to keep the loose dirt from the top side from falling into the well. That piece of pipe was about 1/4 inch thick and weighed a couple of hundred pounds.

Well, my Dad mixed the fertilizer and diesel fuel into a paste and placed it in plastic bread wrappers. He would then tape a stick of dynamite to a long grass rope and then tie a bag of his mixture just below it. Best as I recall he had maybe four sticks of dynamite and four bags of his nitrate mixture tied on that rope.

He and a couple of his friends lowered the rope and the mixture down into the bottom of that well with all the electric caps tied together. There was a long wire that ran the length of the rope. Using the end of this wire above the ground he had spliced it into an extension cord.

Everyone backed off about ten feet and he told me to "Plug it in!" I immediately plugged it into an electrical outlet that was in the 'wash house'. When I plugged it in the entire earth rumbled. As I ran outside of the wash house and around the corner I could see everybody looking up and running for their lives. There was actually a mushroomed shaped cloud coming from within the bowels of the earth.

When I looked up I saw that twenty foot stick of steel pipe way up in the sky. It was so high that it looked no larger than a No. 2 pencil! When it landed it hit the ground less than two feet from the hole from which it was blown. I don't think Mother Earth ever recovered from that explosion, however, she still refused to give up any water that may have been hiding down there.

We went back to toting water in the fall just like always. This went on until the late 1960s or early 1970s when we finally got city water. My father was so excited when they came around selling water meters he bought two!

Now there were four sticks of dynamite left. Proper disposal of those remaining sticks was a job that turned into a mini-adventure for Tommy Dark and I a few years later. While discussing this with my dearly beloved cousin he remains adamant that it was not he who helped me dispose of the left over dynamite even though we used his car to transport the hazardous materials to the appropriate disposal site. He may not remember it because we didn't create any havoc in the neighborhood except for maybe a few hundred fish and a few turtles in Hatchet Creek! Well, heck, it was 'somebody'. Tommy or I may have encountered a temporary memory loss. I am quite sure that through appropriate counseling and therapy or possibly hypnotic regression Tommy will again remember. Anyway the statue of limitations has long since ran out! RD

TD Joins the USAF

November 11th is Veterans Day so I thought I would write a short story. Let's just call it this! Life was much different in the 1960s!

I was just a kid when I joined the Air Force in November of 1966. I dropped out of my short stay in college and there was not much for me in the little town of Kellyton, Alabama where I grew up other than working for my dad which at the time I refused to do. I was having problems at home. I was under the legal age and still drinking way too much. I was headed down the wrong road in life. I had never been in jail but the local State Police knew my car. Plus they knew more about me than they needed to and kept a close watch on me when I hit the highways. I rebelled against everything at the time. I was headed for trouble if I stayed in Kellyton. I needed to get away ASAP. I needed to learn a trade, earn a living and start being independent. I needed to get motivated, set goals for myself and work hard to achieve them. Above all I needed to GROW UP!

Joining one of the military services was part of the process of growing up for most of us young men coming of age back in those days. It certainly was for me in 1966. Some of us saw it as an opportunity and a way to better ourselves but most of us just saw it as a way to get away from our parents and have some adventures on our own and away from home. That is the way it was for me. I joined the Air Force on a cold day in November 1966 and as it later turned out it was the best move I ever made.

The draft was in effect and I received my draft notice with orders to report for induction into the U.S. Army. This was a few months after I turned eighteen and it was the 'luck of the draw for me'. Looking at the Vietnam War Killed in Action listings for 1966 it was mostly Army and Marines! I also noticed that the majority of them were between eighteen and twenty-one. If I was drafted by the Army there was a high probability that I would be one of the names on that list.

By 1967 things in America were in very sad shape. The Vietnam War was only part of the problem but it became the focal point. Our President had lost control, our value system had deteriorated and the whole world seemed to be turned upside down.

It seemed like everyone wanted to pick on those in the military services and blame us for all of those problems. We were heckled, spat at and generally ridiculed in public places mostly at the time these things happened at airports. Most of the action was done by the hippie anti-war protestors. There were many Jane Fonda type people back then. They were very hateful and assertive and they liked to make noise. Everyone else seemed to ignore what they saw happening around them. They just turned away and pretended not to notice. I can honestly say that I preferred being overseas to being in America back in those days of social turmoil. For the first time in my life I was ashamed of the USA!

I wish our leaders would start the process over again and snatch up anyone eighteen years of age who don't ever plan on attending college. Our country would start the long process of getting the way it should be again. All who are eligible should serve at least two years. It did make me change for the better!

When you see a veteran tomorrow tell them thanks for their service. Many my age never had a chance to live a normal life because of actions caused by our government. Heck, many never made it to twenty-one! A war that should have never happened but we went and served and never asked why. Tommy Dark USAF 1966-1970!

I appreciate everyone taking the time to read my story. I thank all the veterans that served in the past. Veterans Day is an official United States holiday that honors people who have served in the U.S. Armed Forces.

As my friend Ed Cook said, while we were in the military we developed bonds with friends that still stand the test of time. To name a few veterans I am still good friends with today, Wayne Branham, Roger Kornegay, Tom Olejniczak, Robert Dark and Merle Strickland are just a few. I salute these friends and Ed Cook for their service.

Even though most of us never knew what impact the military would have in shaping our lives, it did play a very important part as we found out later in life. It took me a few more years after I got out to completely settle down but Tom did finally make it. I also met my wife Jill and never would have if not for the USAF but that's another story!!

In five days from now November 23rd 1966 I left for Lackland Air Force Base Texas. That was forty-eight years ago and I remember it like it was yesterday.

My brother was the only one I could get to take me to Montgomery as my Dad said I was not going to make it in and the Army had me. He had already took me twice and I got sent back because the AF was full. I fooled him as they took me the third time. At that time it was almost impossible to join a branch of the military except the Army and I knew what that would mean. I sweated a little because I only had three days or I was off to the Army but I did finally make it thanks to Charles who never give up on me. It was a time that made young boys grow overnight into young men. What a day that was in November 1966. TD

Brenda Thompson remembers our boys getting drafted and how upset their families were. My brother was one of those and one of the saddest days of my life was seeing him off with my sister-in-law and mother. We all thought he was headed for Viet Nam. He was drafted into the Army and as Tom said that was the worst branch to be drafted in. However, he never left the states and I am thankful for that. Eric, was also drafted into the army and was told he would be in Viet Nam. He too, never left the states. The army did choose his career and turned him to radiology. It was a great career choice for him and still is.

Sandra Clark Patten thanked Tommy for his service and added that she lost a first cousin to that war. Very young and was expecting his first child. Never got to see him. So sad at how those vets were treated.

Leigh Senter remembers her father was in the Army and did two tours in Vietnam. He had four little children and a young wife. He was a gunner on a helicopter the first tour and was Sgt. of an infantry unit during the second tour. He did not talk about his service. We found many metals and certificates after his death in 1999. He was never the carefree, funny dad that he was before going to SE Asia. Salute to all the special vets of that war. They certainly were treated differently on returning than vets today. He stayed in the military for twenty-four years.

Small communities gave up their young and it not only affected the family but the whole town as well that had helped raise them as one of their own. The loss was great!

A Reformed Chicken Thief

I received a call today from my good friend, Kerrie Edwards, from our neighboring state of "Jawja". He was telling me a story about one of his childhood experiences and I thought I would share it here. Seems like when Kerrie was a small boy the family had a great big Pit Bull dog. The dog was the sweetest thing in the world. He loved people and wouldn't hurt a flea. However he had one small flaw and that was he loved to kill chickens. Kerrie's Dad was at his wits end. Every time he turned around that old dog was killing another chicken.

Enough was enough and it was time to teach him a lesson. One day, Kerrie's dad looked out in the yard and sure enough that dog had a rooster on the ground. The feathers were still flying as Kerrie's dad ran around the corner towards the impending rooster massacre. He grabbed that dog by his collar with one hand and the rooster with the other. Knowing the rooster was already dead he began flogging that old dog with the dead rooster. All the time yelling at the dog telling him, "You want a chicken! Here is a chicken that you will never forget".

After meting out what he thought to be sufficient punishment to the dog he threw the rooster on the ground and turned the dog loose. However that rooster wasn't dead! That old rooster jumped up, began flapping his wings and making the most "Gawd-awful" sounds you can imagine. He ran around that dog about three times before scurrying off into the woods. Kerrie says he wished he had a picture of his Dad's face when that half gnawed, fully thrashed rooster stood up. It was a hilarious mixture of disbelief, surprise and humor followed by his trademark exclamation, "We'll I'll be damn!"

From that day forward, every time that dog saw a chicken he would run and hide with his tail tucked between his legs. I don't think it was from the flogging. I think it was from that old rooster somehow coming back to life and causing a mental scar. I guess you could say that the old Pit Bull was now a reformed chicken thief! RD

Basketballs and Ballrooms

If you were a student at Goodwater High School (GHS) prior to 1968 you will remember that all our basketball games were played in the old high school gym. It was not uncommon to have a sellout crowd as the gym had limited seating. I believe two rows down each side of the court and those that they could cram on the stage. The Coosa County Tournament had never been played anyplace other than Coosa County High School in Rockford, the county seat.

It seems as Coosa County High won the tournament every year as their beloved coach, Clyde Ashley, was a good coach. You knew he was a good coach because everyone outside of Rockford disliked him. Even the way he signaled for a timeout was disgusting. In 1963-64 I was told that Coach Gene Hayes had informed the Coosa County Board of Education that Goodwater would not play in the County Tournament unless it was played in Goodwater!

I remember as a ninth grade Agricultural Class member we tore out the old stage and built bleachers in its place that more than tripled the occupancy! I don't remember who won the tournament that year but the winners changed. The tournament alternated between GHS, Weogufka and Rockford. The Coosa County Tournament was the greatest event held in the county. Goodwater started winning their share of the tournaments and I do believe Weogufka won some! In the later years of the old GHS gym we experienced something that was rare! We had basketball games that were rained out. The old gym leaked so bad that the floor would become so wet that it was impossible to play. I remember playing in a football game in Winterboro where it had rained all day and all night. If it had been a basketball game to be played in the GHS gym it would have had to have been postponed. By the way the coach for Winterboro that night was none other than a GHS man, Billy Ray Hatley! Winterboro won!

When I was a senior, class of 1967, the first basketball games in the new gym were the class tournaments. They were always hard fought and I do mean hard fought. Coach Gene Hayes was usually the referee and he would get so red faced due to his anger! Of course we liked that, too!! Coach Hayes was always an excellent math teacher, a good basketball coach and a gentleman! As you may know Coach went to school at FivePoints in Chambers County and was a good basketball player. FivePoints came to GHS for a game.

Junior Bailey, who was an excellent player for GHS and was coached by Gene Hayes brother, Coach James Hayes was playing. Coach was given the task of guarding Junior Bailey man-to-man to try to stop Junior. Junior Bailey scored more points that night than all of the players combined from FivePoints. I liked to kid Mr. Hayes about that in later years. He would still get red faced!!!! CL

James Long remembers that every evening after school they would go to the old gym for practice. Coach Gene Hayes would put us to the test. All who remember the old gym for a basketball game give me an amen. All those who remember the old gym for a game when it was raining give me two amens. All those who remember the open umbrellas for the rain give me three amens. Open umbrellas inside are bad luck which could explain why we never won a game when it rained. Usually after practice we would all load into someones car and go to the Dairy Delite for a coke. Afterward we would walk through town and stop at the corner where the Baptist Church is and hitchhike to Kellyton. I remember Mike Forbus, Steve Lewis, myself, Larry Shivers and Bobby Flournoy were a frequent sight at that corner. The good news is we never had to walk home. Someone would always give us a ride. I used to return the favor but not anymore. Too many crazies in this world. Oh for the good times of those days once again but they too are gone with the wind. However, if you look close at that old corner some late night you might just see some strange boys on that corner hitching a ride. But don't make any effort to stop for them because they left a long time ago!

Betty DeGraffenried Burgess says the old gym was definitely a multipurpose room serving as both gym and auditorium. We held our sock hops and formal dances there. We hung streamers of crepe paper and some old parachutes from the ceiling and thought it looked perfectly beautiful. We had our morning school assembly there at the beginning of each school day. Mr. Westbrook would read the announcements. We would say the pledge of allegiance and then he would call on a student to lead us in prayer. On one very rainy day when the rain was dripping profusely through holes in the roof he called on one boy who was very nervous and shy. The poor thing obviously was so stunned that he just said what many others had said on previous days and as the rain continued to pour through the roof he said, "Dear God, we thank you for this beautiful, sunshiney day...." I don't think any of us dared to snicker!

Two Way Calling

I have never laughed so hard in all of my life. Everyone in Goodwater knew Mr. Gilmer Thomas but knew him as "Roonie." He was a really good fellow and had been an electrician by trade and he loved to talk and carry gossip! He would stop you on the street and talk for as long as you would stay with him. He didn't stutter but he started off every conversation with, "Hey, Hey, Hey, you know what!" Everyone liked to tell him half truths and then he would run with them. Mr. Herman Jacobs the shoe shop man and Mr. Jeff Sprayberry the barber would really pump him full of stuff every morning as he spent a lot of time in both places. I remember everyone liked him and he liked people.

One night about nine pm there were three or four of us in Jimmy Bailey's shop and Jimmy showed us a new device he had acquired. It would allow you to could call two different people at the same time. It also connected those two to the line at the store and we could hear both conversations. This particular night we called Roonie and Mrs. Mac Thomas, Probate Judge Mac Thomas' wife, and they both answered the phone at the same time. Well, finally the two got it straightened out who each other was and talked a few minutes about how they were doing and other matters that usually went on in a conversation. Finally, Mrs. Thomas asked Roonie what he needed and he said he didn't need anything and so Mrs. Thomas inquired about why he had called. Roonie says " Hey, Hey, Hey, you know what? You called me!" This banter went on for several minutes and we were laughing so hard we hurt. Finally, they terminated the call in a nice way but I'm sure they always wondered why the other one called them!

Well then we called two men that did not like each other at all and they had a terrific "cussing" match! It probably made them both feel better as they had wanted to do that a long time. Of course they never figured out why the other one called! We never did that again but it sure was fun! CL

How I lost my first and only job as a Cowboy

I shared a story about taking a wonderful nap one afternoon while working as a cowboy for my Uncle Sam. (Actually, I was just hired to feed the cows a few bales of hay each afternoon). During the second week on the job, I was having so much fun driving that jeep through the pastures that I decided to share some of the fun with Gary Shivers and my cousin Tommy Dark. (We affectionately call Gary "Big G")

One afternoon we met at Uncle Sam's house and the three of us headed across the highway to the pastures in order to feed the cows (and ride, ride, ride). At some point that afternoon, one of us posed the question, "Can you ride a cow like you do a horse?". Well, Big G assured Tommy and I that he could indeed ride a cow. Of course we told him that he couldn't which was all Big G needed to hear.

He tried his best to catch one of those cows, but he just wasn't fast enough. Tommy came up with the bright idea that we could chase the cow with the jeep and when we got close enough, Big G could jump from the jeep onto the cows back. We did and he did. Everyone was having a blast except for the poor old cow. As soon as Big G was on that cow's back, the cow started running wide open. I had no idea they could run so fast. Big G had his arms around that cow's neck and was hanging on for dear life. The cow was running under low hanging tree limbs trying to brush that monkey off its back. Finally the old cow decided to wipe Big G off by running close to a barbed wire fence.

Tommy and I were in hot pursuit in the jeep. When the cow was almost close enough to the fence to shred G's leg off, Big G bailed off. He hit the ground at "Cow-full-throttle" and looked like a tumbleweed rolling across the prairie. Big G was OK. He was just bruised and skinned up about the same amount as he always was during most of his other adventures.

Now that is not why I lost my job as a cowboy. You see my Uncle Sam was a keen observer. He noticed things that never crossed other people's minds. Here is one example that my Dad relayed to me: When my Dad was a young man he didn't have a car of his own. He wanted to carry his girlfriend (my Mom) to the picture show one Saturday night so he asked his oldest brother, Sam, if he could borrow one of his cars.

Sam told my Dad that he could borrow an old Model-A Ford but warned him not to drive it over 35 mph because it was old and tired. Dad borrowed the car, took Mom on the date and returned the car to Sam the next morning. Sam told my Dad not to ask to borrow the car again because he drove the old car too fast. My Dad questioned Sam as to how he knew how fast the car was driven. Sam's reply was, "Look at the bugs on the windshield. Bugs don't splatter like that running 35 mph." Dad said he couldn't argue with that logic.

My last day on the job went something like this: Sam had a gas pump on his property and told me to pump a little gas into the jeep when it needed a drink. After a little over two weeks on the job my Uncle Sam met me as I arrived to pick up the jeep for the daily cow feeding. He said, "Son, I don't need your services any longer. I simply can't afford you." I said, "But Uncle Sam, you are only paying me $5 dollars a week". Sam said, "Its not the $5 dollars that bothers me. My cows are getting skinnier each day and I keep up with the number of gallons of gas that are pumped. According to my calculations, you have put enough gas in that jeep during the past two weeks to drive it to New York City and back twice."

My days as a "Motorized Cowboy" were over. RD

The Candy Bar

I guess I was about ten or so and Grannie and I had gone to town to 'trade' as old folks are wont to say. Grannie didn't drive, never did, so I'm guessing mom drove us. When ever we went anywhere there was always a few items that went along with us. One was Grannie's spit can. This was an old can that had held some food item long ago eaten and washed out and half filled with dirt so she could dip her snuff and have a place to spit. She had dipped pretty much all her life and I can remember some kisses when I was younger that had a decided 'snuffy' taste to them. Fortunately she gave the habit up later on in life. I was thankful as was all of the other kids that came up after me. The other item was a jug of ice water. She would fill it up before we left even if it was just down the road. Down the road being a relative term. That could be anything from a few miles to half a days hard driving! This was before the days of bottled water and most service stations, yes they did provide service back then, usually had a sign to the effect of 'Fill your jugs for free'! Seems Grannie wasn't the only one that had a jug in the car. This did include ice. Try getting that today!

Anyway I got side tracked there. Grannie had some business to transact at one of the stores in town and I begged off to stay at the grocery where she would return and do her shopping. I have no idea where Mom was. So while Grannie was off doing her thing I was just wandering around the store looking at all the wonders for sale. Then it hit me. I had inadvertently wandered into the candy aisle and the aroma of the various chocolate delights overwhelmed me! Being financially embarrassed as I was back then I resorted to the only means available to me. That is getting a candy bar using the five finger discount method. I though I was so cool that I would never get caught. Wrong! The manager person was sitting up in his office loft that was raised up a few feet off the floor near the cash registers. Gave him an unfair advantage if you ask me, kinda like a hunter in a tree stand if you will! Anyway I was busted as I tried to make my exit without paying. Caught Milky Way handed if you will.

So the guy takes me up into his manager loft and starts reading me the riot act. Threatens to turn me over to the police. I can live with that. The worse thing this man can do to me is turn me over to Grannie! I guess I should have pleaded temporary insanity as I had been overcome by the chocolate fumes and was obviously impaired! He asks where my folks are and I tell him downtown and they will be back soon. I promise to never do it again. I swear I will just go to the car and wait till time to go home if he will just let me go. Somewhere along about this time I see Grannie coming in the door. This elevated loft office thing does have its advantages! I slump down in my seat and fortunately she walks by none the wiser. The manager and I come to an agreement, I give the candy back (like I had a choice), promise to never do it again and he'll let me go with a stern warning about jail time if he ever catches me again. Well, dude, if I decide to steal more candy you can bet your sweet behind I will dang sure be more careful next time and you will not catch me! Pretty much the mindset of all criminals I guess.

He lets me go, I sneak out and wait in the car. Grannie is none the wiser and I have never told this tale till now. By the way I never stole anymore candy but I still look over my shoulder when I'm eating a Milky Way! PGG

Insect Control

I attended the Kellyton Methodist Church each Sunday until I left for military service in 1966. Most of those years were spent in the old original wooden structure (Not sure when it was built). That church was later torn down and a new brick church was built. I remember that the church had no air conditioning, nor did it even have fans of any type to assist in cooling. We simply opened the several windows that lined both sides of the sanctuary. These were open windows with no screens.

During the summer and early fall months these open windows allowed all manner of flying insects to enter and sometimes fly freely among the congregation during the service. Even though these insects rarely caused problems we had one good church member who apparently felt it was his civic duty to alleviate as many distracting pests as possible.

This leads us to an elderly gentleman named Mr. Madison Gilliland. We could always count on Mr. Madison to be at church every Sunday. We could also count on Mr. Madison to sit in the exact same place every Sunday (left side of the sanctuary, two pews back from the front on the left end of the pew). Another thing we could always count on was that Mr. Madison always came armed for insect control. He always had a pair of scissors in his coat pocket. As was common wasp (we called them "Wost") would make their way through the open windows, fly around for a bit and then land on the inside of the windows or perhaps the wall next to the windows.

It mattered not if the choir was singing or the preacher was speaking or a testimony was being given, Mr. Madison was on a mission. He constantly monitored the windows and the walls. When he caught a glimpse of the dreaded wasp or yellow jacket that had stopped to rest he would get out of his pew and walk over to the menacing varmint and simply "cut it in half" and then return to his seat.

I have personally witnessed him roaming around and neutralizing a dozen or so invaders on any given Sunday. Occasionally, one of those "Wost" would actually sting an individual who might panic when the unwanted villain happened to land on them. This caused much consternation amongst the congregation, particularly for Mr. Madison! "Wost" stings in those days was treated immediately on the spot usually by applying some tobacco spit. RD

Friday the 13th

Today, as you know, is Friday the 13th. In 1965 I had just graduated from Auburn and had bought my first car. It was a navy blue Chevy Malibu from Dyas Chevrolet in Auburn and I was beginning my teaching career in Pensacola, Florida. At that time Florida teachers were on a ten-month contract so my job began on August 16th. Alabama teachers didn't report for duty until their one day of teachers' institute the Friday before Labor Day. Mama still had another two or three weeks of summer vacation and she wanted to ride down with me to see where I would be living and teaching. The plan was that she would ride the bus back home a few days later.

My roommates and I had leased a house in Pensacola and were set to move in on Friday the 13th of August. Mama was superstitious and tried to convince me that this was not a good plan. The stars were not in our favor to move on this very unlucky day. I, of course, poo-poohed her objections, noting that a friend of mine planned to get married that same Friday the 13th. If she wasn't worried about having a wedding on that date then I sure wasn't worried about moving to Pensacola either. So off we went with the car packed to the gills with all of my stuff and barely enough room for me and Mama to squeeze inside.

All went well until we were a few miles past Atmore where we had stopped to have a Coke. One of my roommates from Selma had met us in Montgomery and she was following behind us. It began raining and the roads were slick. I hit a bad spot, began hydro-planing and lost control of my brand new car (which had just a few hundred miles on it). We eventually wound up across the road in the middle of a forest of trees owned by International Paper Company. I just had to select which tree I was going to crash into. There was no way I could avoid hitting one or more of them!

I did center a tree and Mama's head went through the windshield. The steering wheel kept me from the same result. There were no such things as seat belts to protect us back then. Thankfully my roommate Beba was right behind us so she could flag down another car to go and call for help. This was also decades before anybody even thought of cell phones. Mama was hurt badly and her face was bleeding profusely. I was in a lot of pain as well but obviously was not as seriously injured as she was.

The ambulances finally arrived and transported both of us to Sacred Heart Hospital in Pensacola. Mama had a broken neck and required about 150 stitches in her face. I just had a couple of cracked ribs which were painful but, of course, nothing nearly as serious as what Mama had.

She wound up staying in Sacred Heart Hospital for over six weeks. She had to be in traction for a long time and finally progressed to wearing a neck brace. The news that reached Goodwater was much more dismal. The report got out that she was paralyzed from the neck down and would never be able to walk again. She finally returned to Goodwater in early October but I don't think she returned to Goodwater High until either after Thanksgiving or Christmas that year. Our sweet friend Elinor Roberts filled in for her as a permanent substitute for several months.

When Mama packed to go to Pensacola, she had put in some shorts and a swimsuit since we were planning to go to the beach while she was visiting us. She said that if anybody in the hospital looked in her suitcase and saw those items they would send her to the psych ward! Nobody in their right mind would pack those items for a stay in the hospital!

She eventually made a full recovery. When she was told about nine or ten months later that she could take off the neck brace she said she had gotten so dependent on it that she wasn't sure she could hold her head up without it. The scars on her face faded very quickly. A few years later, she began noticing that something was irritating her cheek. Dr. Cockerham discovered that a sliver of glass from the windshield had been sewn up in her cheek. It had apparently been deeply imbedded and it took a few years to work its way up to the surface where it could finally be removed.

From that day on, Mama took serious precautions on Friday the 13th. She once declared, "The only way I will ever get hurt on Friday the 13th again will be from falling out of my own bed because I will NEVER go ANYWHERE else on Friday the 13th again!"

So, y'all take Mama's advice and be careful out there today!
BDB

The Sermon

I should have been whipped! As a youth and a member of the Goodwater Presbyterian Church it was required that you go to Sunday School, church services, Senior High Fellowship, Sunday Night Services and choir practice on Wednesday night. Yes I had to sing in the choir and my cousin Scotty (Anne Rogers Agnew) and I could bring tears to your eyes with our singing. We had a preacher that we were all so fond of and he would pay a lot of attention to us. He was just a good friend to everyone and he picked at Scotty and me a lot.

Anyway, after Sunday School we went to the church basement and put on our choir robes and got our sheet music and placed the music in a really nice black book. I guess that was to make us look like pros! Just before going in the sanctuary we lined up as to how we would sit in the choir loft. I was last because I sat on the back row. When we entered the sanctuary the music was being played by Mrs. Dorothy (Diane Robbins Pegues). The congregation had their heads bowed in meditation as did the preacher. As we were entering the choir loft we had to march behind the pulpit to gain entrance to the choir area. I was last and I saw that Brother Clyde had his sermon typed out and was placed in the big pulpit bible that was open and ready! I thought it would be interesting to see how good a job Brother Clyde could do without his sermon notes. As his head was bowed in meditation I took the sermon and placed it in my sheet music folder and entered the choir as usual!

When he returned to the pulpit he looked in the shelf just under the top of the pulpit and behind him in the chair he had just left! He knew something was wrong but he had no clue as to where his sermon had gone. Church service was really short that day! He didn't mention that for several years! Brother Clyde being a bit devious did try to bait the culprit by placing a folder in the Bible as bait. However I could see the sermon in his hand as his head was bowed in meditation on future Sundays. He never mentioned it to me but he did to several people and they just laughed and they all accused me of doing it! No proof was forth coming and I never admitted it till this day. So Brother Clyde, if you are still with us I want you to know it was a really good sermon and I still love you!
CL

Gambler's Chalk

Back in about 1963, when I was in the 10th grade at Goodwater High School, several of the boys discovered the fine art of "Throwing Dice". No, we didn't play "Craps" because none of us knew how. We would throw "High Dice". Whomever could throw the highest numbers won the nickel, dime or quarter. The principal, Mr. Wesbrook, caught wind of this and raided the restrooms and other usual hiding places constantly in an effort to thwart this evil practice. Over a short period of time he amassed quite a collection of "Dice". He called a general assembly and read everyone the riot act on the evils of gambling. He threatened expulsion, calling our parents (which was almost a certain death sentence) and all other types of punishment.

There was a certain group from Kellyton, Alabama that refused to be outdone by his threats. One of the gang, I think it was my cousin Tommy Dark, had found a large piece of white chalk (remember blackboards?). Anyway, he broke the chalk in half and began to carefully make these little squares that resembled "Dice" by rubbing the chalk on the sidewalk. After a little work with a Number 2 pencil the dies had the required number of dots on each side. The ingenious idea behind this was that if we were threatened with a raid we could simply drop them on the ground and crush the evidence!

Many of the Kellyton Gang took typing in the 10th grade under Mrs. Preston Nail. Since she loved us all we could get by with clustering together in the back of the room. In those days, the typing textbook was a long book (I believe it was blue in color). Anyway, there were about four of us; Tommy Dark, Mike Ogburn, maybe Larry Dennis and of course yours truly clustered together during typing class. We had sort of made us a "Dice Throwing Area" in the back by standing our typing books on edge and bouncing the dice off of them. We had a little Las Vegas going on when all of a sudden the dreaded principal Mr. C. O. Westbrook (COW), comes through the door of the classroom. He immediately saw us clustered up with the typing books on edge and made a bee-line to our table.

Mike Ogburn scooped up the chalk dice and put them in his mouth. He started chewing them and then a big swallow. The evidence was gone but Mike began getting a little green around the gills. Mr. Westbrook wanted to know what we were doing. We said, "Group Study". He looked sternly at Mike who had the tell-tale white around his lips and told him to open his mouth. He said, "What were you chewing on?" Mike told him that it was Rolaids because he had an upset stomach.

We got by with that one, but it scared us so bad that I don't think any of the gang ever played dice again! Well at least not at Goodwater High School. Ah, the fun we had as kids!

Now its clear to the whole world that Tommy Dark was indeed the mastermind of the entire gambling underworld at Goodwater High School. At the time, I thought that him asking me to carve dice from chalk was an innocent endeavor and had no idea that they were to be used in anything except perhaps a game of Monopoly. Finally, it became clear to me that my dear cousin was headed down a rough and rocky path. I felt the need to intercede! I did and if it were not for my heartfelt guidance there is no telling how that young soul would have turned out. Stealing Buicks no doubt! RD

Tommy adds a few things to this story. Mr Robert P. Dark was the mastermind in making these chalk dice. I think I came up with the idea of using chalk. We could just toss them on the floor and if caught they would turn to white dust when stepped on and crushed. I just needed someone to do the art work and Robert had that talent like none other. I remember him taking lots of time making the tiny dots on the dice with a real ink pen. They looked like the real deal.

We were now set and our backup plan would work. If only we had camera phones back then! I can see Mike's face now as it had a red glow to it after eating those dice. He did not have time to crush them as planned so in his mouth they went. I never tasted chalk and maybe it would sure cure some things. It did that day. It cured us from getting our rear ends red! TD

Charles says this is a brilliant story and a really smart scheme to out do the system and of course that system was the COW system. His discipline was so important in our development and we have to appreciate it now. We had to wear socks, belt, shirt tucked in and your slacks had to pass the golf ball test. This test was putting a golf ball under the waist of your pants and letting the ball drop to the floor! If it stopped due to your pants being too tight you had to go home and get another pair on! The tough part was having two pair of pants! Of course, your hair length was required to make you look like a young man!

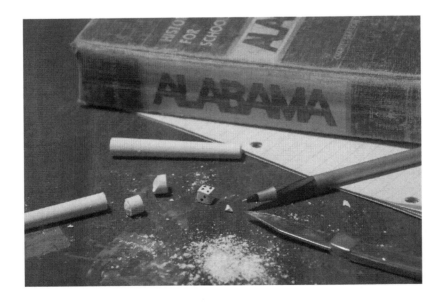

Plowing the Garden

My parent's first garden as a married couple started out simply enough. My folks were married in May, 1946. Like many newlyweds, they rented a room in a community member's home until sometime in 1948. At some point, my Dad had arranged to purchase a couple of acres and began building their first home. Dad told me that they were so proud of their new home and couldn't wait to have their first garden. They decided to plow a small spot behind the house for a small garden. The only problem was that they didn't have a tractor or a mule nor the money to pay someone to break up this new ground for the garden. I recall that he borrowed a "Push-Plow" from his father-in-law. The plan was to use it to break the ground for planting

He said that he worked for most of one day and had only plowed an area that was about the size of a large feather pillow. He then got the bright idea that if he ran a chain from the back bumper of their 1939 Plymouth through the steel wheel on the push-plow he would, in effect have a 'tractor'. He would need someone to drive the Plymouth and someone to handle the plow.

Now he had been teaching my mom to drive with somewhat limited success. However, she was still having a bit of trouble with the clutch/accelerator ratio in order to ensure a smooth take-off. It seemed like such a great plan, at least on paper. Dad was behind the plow and my Mom was the designed 'tractor' driver. After several 'false starts' with Mom letting out on the clutch too soon and the engine dying, then not applying the correct amount of accelerator pressure and making the car jerk my Dad was becoming somewhat frustrated. Finally he yelled,"Give it some doggone gas" or something to that effect! That's when my mom pressed the accelerator pedal-to-the-metal and took her foot of the clutch. Dad said that that Plymouth took off like a rocket ship. He was running trying to keep up and the plow was throwing dirt high into the air! They were plowing!

Then it happened. The plow hit a big rock and stopped dead still. Dad said that plow threw him about ten feet straight up. Mom was not deterred and kept going without ever even looking back. Dad was lying face down in the garden spot and Mom dragged that plow over to the neighbor's land before she was able to stop that Plymouth. That pretty much ended the gardening project for that year. RD

Spankings!

I know most of you have never had a spanking and it's pretty much frowned upon nowadays. I have often wondered how Tommy Dark and his cousin Robert Dark survived with all of their goings on. I got a lot of them but I believe this was the worse one I ever, ever got. My sister, Martha, even thought it was bad enough that she laughed. Laughing at your sibling getting whacked was enough to get one of your own! Charlie Smith echoes that if he ever laughed at a whipping his brother or sister was getting he would get one twice as hard and twice as long.

My cousin, Scott Rogers, had spent the night with me and when we were kids that was a big thing and it was pretty much automatic trouble. This particular night after supper I asked my mother if Scotty (at that time called Jimmy) and I could go to the movie show and see "Sink the Bismarck," or something like that and she told me, "Go and ask your daddy". Well, I forgot to ask him as I knew he would be in bed before eight o'clock and he was. I ask my mother again and she wanted to know what my daddy had said. I hem-hawed around and evaded the question and sorta indicated that it was okay with him.

So, we need a quarter each to go to the movie and get some popcorn and a coke and she scrounged around and gave us the money. Off we went and I felt so clever by out smarting my folks. We went in and paid Mr. Frank Nail our fifteen cents for admission and then we got us a bag of popcorn and a coke. We were ready to relax and enjoy the show. All was well with the world.

We had been sitting there for several minutes enjoying the show, the coke and the popcorn. It was all good. I had put some popcorn in my mouth and as I tilted my head back for a drink of the Coke all I could see was my dad standing there absent a smile on his face. I feebly smiled back and to my dismay he didn't! He told me it was time to go home and without question Scotty and I immediately vacated our comfortable seats and hustled home being followed by my dad.

Well when we got in the front door of the house he never even stopped to say hello to the rest of the family. He just grabbed me by my arm (boy I wished their had been a Department of Human Resources back then) and led me to the back room and made a brief statement to me about telling lies.

He snatched his belt off and I can still remember the sound of the last four inches of that belt coming out of the belt loops. I always hated that sound as it meant sheer doom.

Well, he whipped my butt to a fair-thee-well. I cried and tried to out run him to no avail doing the 'circle dance'! He had my arm in one hand and the belt in the other. We were going in a circle but he kept up with me and kept whipping my little butt. After about fifteen lashes he stopped and asked me if I had learned my lesson and I couldn't even respond as I was crying so hard. Also I had those crying hiccups and he kept saying, "Dry up! Dry up! Say! Say!" and then this went on for several seconds. I finally caught my breath and responded, "YES SIR"! He replied, "Well you better have!"

That's when I made the mistake of asking if we could go back to the movie! I can tell you that was not a good question at that particular time. Here we go again! I learned my lesson for a second time that night. After I finally dried up as dad said, Scotty and I were planning another adventure! Surely he wouldn't get up twice in the same night. We did not go back to the show and he did not get up again that night. It really was not as bad as it sounds. It was just a typical day for us! It was nothing as bad as getting initiated to Letter Club (G-Club). Scotty and I got that the same day too. We were pretty much accustomed to that by then though! CL

Spankings Part Two

When we were kids and the other siblings got a spanking we didn't laugh. This is one time I should have kept my mouth shut! The worse rule to break was to wake up one of our parents during an after lunch nap. My sisters and I were laying on a bed laughing and cutting up and I was between the two. We were really loud and we thought everything was going fine when our old man burst through the door. He already had a switch that had been stripped of leaves and started giving us a thrashing. Immediately my sister, Martha Gray, started crying and I was not feeling the switching as I was between my sisters plus I had a bead spread over me as they did also. Anyway, when he finished the whipping everyone was crying and I was crying a fake cry and he left the room with firm instructions to keep quiet.

A few seconds after he shut the door I started that nah, nah, nah it didn't hurt me ha, ha, ha, ha chant. I should have kept my mouth shut and just silently laughed because the door was again firmly opened and I was taken out of the bed and was given a good whipping and I really did cry this time. Those switches could make you dance. A belt was not near as bad as a switch. We had a handy bush at the back door that provided switches and finally died from the lack of leaves and branches. If I had been smarter I would have killed that bush a long time ago. My sisters had quit crying and by now they were laughing. I guess that was just fair play. CL

Betty DeGraffenried Burgess adds that she also got plenty of spankings too. Once Mama got a green switch from the yard and whipped my legs. Since the switch was green and my legs were very white it made whelps on my legs which looked pretty bad. When Daddy came home and saw my legs he told Mama that he never thought he would see my legs looking like that. She said that was the only time my granddaddy ever said a word one way or the other when they were having an argument. Apparently granddaddy said that he had seen the switching and it was not nearly as bad as it looked and that if I didn't learn to mind Mama then (I was probably four or five) that I never would and that was the end of that. Our children got spankings too, by the way.

Charles Dunham relates the worst part of his Mama giving him a whipping was she would make him go cut the peach limb! I was about ten or so and Mama sent me to get a switch because I had dared to do something to Annette, my younger and only sister! Mama didn't let anybody do anything to her and get by with it. Now everyone knows that I was so nice and sweet and would never be mean to her or to my baby brother Larry. I go get the smallest limb on the tree and bring it back to Mama. She sternly says to me "go get a good switch " (which I thought was an oxymoron)!

As I was hustling back to the peach tree my mind was going ninety to nothing! What can I possibly do to help this situation? Then out of the blue I have the solution! I cut a good-sized switch with my trusty pocket knife which every red blooded boy had. Then I cut nearly half way through the switch when I was carefully trimming the limbs off. Now when Mama started whipping me the switch would break in two! End of story! Not quite!

Mama inspected the switch and saw the halfway cut and for some unknown reason she got "mad as a Jap"! She borrowed my knife and cut her own switch which was a good one! Then she proceed to beat the meanness out of me and I was such a sweet boy! That whipping was one to remember!

Robert Dark tells this one! When I was about thirteen or so I had the idea that since I was now a teenager I was smarter than most folks especially my parents. I smarted off to my Mom and as always she said, "Go get me a switch". I went out to the edge of the woods and I came back with a switch about the size of a match stick and about twelve inches long. Mama had fire in her eyes as she told me to get myself back outside and bring her a real switch.

This time I brought in one that was still the size of match stick but was maybe eighteen inches long. She informed me that I had better get a good switch and added "You just wait until your Daddy gets home". Being my little smart-butt self this time I came back with a stick about three feet long and as big around as a quarter. In a sarcastic way I said, "Is this what you had in mind?" She said, "Yep, that's the one" and round and round in a circle we went. There is no escape from a circle whuppin! That's when your mama has got you by one arm and is flogging your fanny with the other and you are trying to get away but you can only go around in a circle.

I learned a valuable lesson that day. My Mom is eighty-seven now and I feel sure that if I said or did something to warrant it she would tell me to go cut her a switch. You can bet it would be a proper sized switch the first time!

Clyde Goes to the Hospital

Clyde Worthy was an old, shrivelled up fellow that had no fear of any man. He lived a tough but simple life and if he any job skills other than making moonshine I didn't know any of them. Clyde not only lived a rough life but he lived a tough life and I don't really know if it was his choice or just the way the cards fell. We all know that we have a lot of choices in life and for the most part we had guidance in making those choices. Due to my church life and family guidance I always knew right from wrong and regretfully I did not always make the right choice. I learned that bad choices presented bad results and bad punishment that was not always by the belt! Back to Clyde!

I don't guess Clyde really had a home that he could depend on until his last years and I'm glad that Melinda and I didn't take that away from him. He loved where he lived even though none of us would enjoy his life style. Clyde's last days began on a Wednesday night before Thanksgiving. Melinda was working in Dadeville and it was dark thirty when she got home every night with our new child Chase. This particular night as I was preparing supper Melinda arrived home with Chase and I was really excited to see both of them. Thanksgiving was the next day with the family coming to our house for Thanksgiving dinner. Melinda informed me that she had seen Clyde crawling across the driveway pulling a fire log and looked pretty bad. That night it was raining and had turned cold so that alone concerned me about Clyde's situation.

I put on my jacket and went down to Clyde's house and could see through his window that he had fallen back on his bed with the piece of firewood. I jimmied the door and got in his house to find Clyde in pretty bad shape and cold. I couldn't get a sensible response from him as I am sure that he had failed to take his prescribed medicine and to top it off he had on six pairs of pants! All wet and not from the rain!

Turning around I noticed Artis Whetstone had appeared and hollered "Praise the Lord you are here." I don't know where Artis came from but he sorta helped look after Clyde. I might add that Artis Whetstone was one of the finest men I have ever known. Artis and I were both able to get Clyde down to one pair of pants that was dry even though not clean.

Artis asked what were we going to do now? I told Artis that I was going to take Clyde to the hospital because he needed help and I doubted he would live until morning in the shape he was in. I picked Clyde up like a small child and carried him and put him in the front seat of my car. As I was leaving Artis was on the front porch chanting,"Praise the Lord, Praise the Lord".

Admitting Clyde to the hospital was rather comical and interesting. First they inquired if Clyde was my father and I told them no it was my wife's father! Finally I told them who he was and why I brought him in and that he was on Medicare or Medicaid and if I had to pay the deductible I would. They admitted Clyde and he came around pretty fast as I was leaving he was ready to go home. After a few minutes I convinced Clyde he needed to stay and let these folks get him well. He finally agreed and I went home to help Melinda get ready for Thanksgiving!

That Thanksgiving night my neighbor Wayne Carr and I went to the hospital to check on Clyde. I had bought Clyde some new socks, underwear, clothes and some toilet articles like shaving cream and a double-edged razor but no toothpaste as Clyde was toothless! He was actually glad to see us and that made us both happy. I informed Clyde that we were there to shave his seven day old whiskers that were like a steel brush! He readily agreed and said he really needed a shave. Thankfully, Wayne volunteered to shave Clyde and after four razor blades and about thirty minutes Wayne had Clyde shaved except for about 3/4 of an inch all the way around his mouth. Now remember Clyde didn't have any teeth and his mouth had sunk in a good bit! Laughingly, Wayne said you can do the rest! I told him if he would shave him I would get his mouth in a position to shave! There was a box of surgical gloves in Clyde's room so I got a pair of them on and I told Clyde what I was going to do and Clyde actually chuckled! With the gloves on I reached in and pulled Clyde's lips out like a hooked fish and Wayne finished the job! Clyde actually looked handsome.

He stayed in the hospital for about a week. One night out of that week we didn't go see Clyde and the next night he sternly inquired as to our where abouts last night with a tear or two trickling down his cheek. When it was time for Clyde to get out of the hospital a nurse called me and told me that Clyde needed to go to a rest home. He was not able to take care of himself and I knew right then and there that was going to be a problem.

I went to the hospital thinking of what I could tell Clyde about where he needed to go and not use the word rest home. Entering Clyde's room I informed him that he was going to have to spend a little time in a nursing home such that he could get well quicker. He surprisingly agreed that he would do that but he wasn't going to no rest home or old folks home. I told him that I didn't blame him. The hospital had done a excellent job and had found Clyde a bed at Goodwater Nursing Facility. CL

Shelling Peas for Votes

I hate to tell political campaign stories but this was a pretty good one. Back in 1978 when I ran for public office for the first time I really didn't know what to say or how to act. I guess I did a pretty good job as I won! I remember it was in the middle of July and it was hot and I was on the trail and campaigning on the Lay Dam road. I stopped at the next house as usual and knocked on the front door and then heard a voice saying come to the back yard and I did.

There were three people sitting in a small circle in the shade of an old oak tree shelling butter beans. One man and two women and the man was married to one of the women and the other was her sister. I stated by business and purpose for the visit and was then handed a dish pan about half full of un-shelled green butter beans. If you have never shelled green butterbeans it won't mean much to you. I think they had been shelling the mature beans and saving those for a visitor!

Well, I was trying to get three votes so I commenced to shelling those darn green butterbeans and went through an interrogation as if I was trying to be the Secretary of Defense. They would ask questions about capital punishment, voters rights and questions I never dreamed that three folks out in the country could come up with! Thankfully, same sex marriage was not an issue then! They had enough questions that took so long to answer that I shelled everyone of those butterbeans and had turned my thumb green.

Seeing that I had finally finished the man dropped the bomb on me. He said "Luker, if we were registered to vote you would be our man!" I'm glad he had taken the dish pan full of shelled butter beans before this announcement or I would have thrown them out in the yard. Campaigning is really interesting. I had one woman come to answer the door that had on nothing but her nitroglycerin patch. No! I didn't know what to say! It actually scared me! CL

M-80s and the Christmas Play

Back in the early to mid 1960s, Kellyton United Methodist Church finally tore down the old wooden church building and built a new brick building. I sure missed that old church house. It had no air conditioning in the summer and even less heat in the winter.

The first Christmas play in that new church was on a rainy Sunday night just a few days before the 25th of December. Since the building was new not all the landscaping had been completed. There was no grass close to the building. It was just that old sticky red clay all around the building which Alabama has an abundance of.

The play was the traditional type that many churches put on at Christmas time. It was a typical creche scene with Mary, Joseph, Baby Jesus and of course the three Wise Men. It kicked off at seven pm on schedule but there was a problem!

It seems that some of the teenaged boys of the church had gotten their hands on some M-80 firecrackers. In those days real M-80 firecrackers were roughly the equivalent to 1/4 stick of dynamite. They had a green waterproof fuse and would actually explode under water but that's another story. It had been discovered by some of those boys that you could light a cigarette and stick the fuse of that M-80 into the side of the cigarette. By doing this you had a time delay of sorts for the firecracker.

Now the teenaged boys in that small country church pretty much consisted of Tommy Dark, (Tommy-Boy), Gary Shivers (Big G), Mike Ogburn (Big O), Larry Shivers and of course yours truly. At least one, maybe two, of the above mentioned individuals had devised three cigarette timed M-80 fuses just prior to the play starting. These were placed by them right next to the back side of the church.

The play started on time and the three wise men came down the center aisle all dressed in their robes and turbans and such. About the time they reached the stage the first one of the time bombs went off!

Kaaaaaboooommmm! The windows of that new building rattled almost to the point of breaking. All the church members were startled and were looking at each other wondering what in the world had happened.

Then just a few minutes later Kaaaaaabooooooommmmm! The second M-80 went off.

One of the deacons, Mr. Robert Culberson (rest his soul), got up and walked out the front door of the church to investigate. He surveyed the situation and walked around to the rear of the church to have a look. Just about that time (You guessed it) Kaaaaaaabooooooommm! The final one went off!

Shortly, Mr. Culberson opened the door of the church and when he came in he was covered with red clay mud from head to foot. He had a dazed look on his face and looked a tad bit pitiful. Seems that during his investigation of the situation he had seen the glow of a burning cigarette. Now he knew that no one was supposed to be out and about the rear of the church and went to investigate. About the time he got close to it the thing had went off.

We persevered and finished the play but when I got home my parents gave me a grilling that would make water boarding look like child's play. I never broke and apparently neither did any of the other boys in spite of our parents threats of sentencing us to life-long grounding and even spending time in the electric chair.

To this day, I will not intentionally admit to having anything to do with this sordid episode. However if I were pressed really hard I would tell you that my incorrigible cousin Tommy Dark probably had something to do with it. RD

The Old Kellyton United Methodist Church

Coming Home

I almost forgot. Forty four years ago today I walked into the courthouse in Ishpeming Michigan, paid the required $5 and married my wife. Then off to Alabama we headed. We only had $400 to our name, no place to live and no jobs but it worked. We only had the $400 because I sold her car as we did not want to drive two to Alabama. It was a 1966 Ford Mustang six cylinder automatic with very few miles on it. She still misses her car. I am glad she put up with me for all those years. I had a new 1970 Road Runner so we took the best of the two. I later had to sell the Road Runner because Jill had problems driving a stick shift.

My daughter in law asked me today how I come to ask Jill to marry me. I told her the truth. I had to much to drink that night! As Monk Hayes used to tell me when I played cards at the Elks Club back in the 1970s, "Yall watch out, Dark has had some of that nervevene medicine!"

Jill kept asking me if there were a lot of snakes in Alabama. I told her, "Yes, many!" There are no poisonous snakes in the Upper Peninsula of Michigan and that was one of her fears going south. Of course being the fool that I am I told her she had to be careful because they would jump out of trees on her. We spent our second night at Lookout Mountain Tennessee. As we walked all around the area I kept looking up in the trees trying to scare her. She would jump when I told her there was one up in that tree.

I would have never in a million years have went to that little place in Ishpeming Michigan that night in April 1970 if not for my good friend Tom Olejniczak. He and I were just young airman trying to find something to do on the weekend. He suggested we go to Ishpeming that night. Heck, I could not even spell that name but I said let's go. I met Jill that night in April of 1970 and we started dating until we married December 7th. Thanks to Tom for the idea that night. Life works in strange ways. TD

Robert Dark relates the story how he also tried to pull one over on his wife. Right before I got out of the Air Force, my (then) wife and I were talking about what I was going to do for a job. We were home for a weekend (from Tyndall AFB in Florida) and were continuing our discussion one night while driving to Alex City for a bite to eat.

Just as we were approaching the old "Pines Motel", I told her that Bo Gunn had offered me a night job at the Motel. She asked, "What kind of job". I told her that he would pay me $2.50 per hour for turning that flashing "Pines Motel" sign on and off every few seconds. She got all concerned and worried that I might get bored!

The Road Runner

Watermelons and Flat Tires

It being the Fourth of July and all I went into a market the other day and picked up a watermelon in one hand. It was several dollars for this melon. Now when I was a kid I could not pick up a watermelon with one hand or two hands for that matter. It took both arms and holding it close to my chest. Now that was a watermelon!

Now I bring this up to relate my foray (a very brief foray) into watermelon farming. I was about fourteen or so at the time and was a member of the FFA, that's Future Farmers of America, for those amongst the readers who may be undereducated. I knew that watermelons were a cash crop and were pretty much easily grown or so I thought. I, being the great agricultural intellect that I was back then, decided that I would be a watermelon farmer and pretty much be set for life.

The first thing that I determined was fertilizer was expensive and I had this embarrassing financial problem. Not to be deterred I knew from my studies with FFA that organic fertilizer such as wood chips, sawdust and cow manure could be used. Most of these could be had for free. You just had to know where it was and have access to it. Well, I knew where there was all the sawdust you could ask for, you just had to go get it. My father had run this small sawmill for a while and there was a big bunch of sawdust there. I devised a plan. Now we didn't have a tractor to plow this field and with my part timers I don't remember if we still had George the horse to plow the field either. I didn't say it was a good plan! I am usually good at plans, just not so much on the follow through but that's another story. There was this perfect area behind the house for a watermelon patch. I talk my father into using the old pickup to go get the sawdust and he is agreeable. Don't know what that is all about as he had never agreed to any of my superior plans before. I must be onto something! I enlisted the assistance of my boyhood friend Bobby and we are on the way. Drive the few miles to the sawdust pile and load the truck and drive back and unload it and spread it around. Now I am somewhat amazed as to how little an area a pickup truck full of sawdust will cover. I was figuring on two, maybe three loads at the most and here we are with barely the corner of the field covered. And I am talking about a very small corner. So, being the optimistic entrepreneurs we were we went for the second load. It would obviously spread out more! This is where the flat tire comes in.

On the way there we somehow develop a flat. Now this in itself is not unusual as most of the tires we had on almost all of the vehicles we owned at the time you could see air showing through! I remember going to the trash piles in the local community to 'shop' for tires. People would throw away tires that were better than the ones we had and we would recycle them. We were 'green' even back then but we just didn't know it! Nothing to do but change it out.

We usually had not one but two or more spares or more due to the aforementioned air showing through thing. Well, this was not the case today. We had spares but they were flatter than the tire on the truck. No cell phones or such back then so the only recourse was to take one of the spare tires and get it fixed. When I say get it fixed I mean we had to fix it. No place in our little community to get a flat fixed plus that embarrassing financial thing I mentioned earlier!

In order to accomplish the same we had to take the tire back home where we had patches and a hand pump and such. I did mention that the sawdust pile was a few miles away didn't I? I may not have mentioned it but it was about ninety degrees or so. Well, a few hours later and several miles of walking and carrying and rolling a tire we have the truck ready to go again. It is late afternoon. And hot. And we are dead tired. We go home. That one small area that was covered with sawdust grew a wonderful patch of weeds.

I bought the watermelon and was happy to pay the price!
PGG

Running Out of Gas and the Scary Movie

It was the Fall of 1963 and I had been driving (legally) for a few months and every now and then my parents would let me take the family car to go see a movie. Most of the time I had to carry my brother Timmy-Boy with me. He is almost five years younger than me and when you are sixteen you sure don't want an eleven year old kid cramping your style. Now the 'borrow the car tonight' rules were pretty simple. Be home by 10:00 pm. That didn't mean 10:15, it didn't mean 10:05, it meant no later than 10:00 pm! Period!

One Friday night I was lucky enough to get to go to the movie without having my brother tag-along. I went to the Strand Theater in Alex City and the movie "Blood Feast" was showing. It was the first movie that I had ever seen that was filled with blood and guts. It actually came with a warning about parents letting young impressionable males see the film! It was a very low grade movie and the acting was terrible. Since this was my first real horror movie it upset me very much and I just knew I would have nightmares about all that gore.

After the movie I made a couple of laps around Buck's Springhill Dairy Queen as was the custom. After the last circle I did the obligatory burn-out as I left and headed home. I was well within my 10:00 pm curfew. All was well until I ran out of gas less than a mile from home. I knew I shouldn't have done that burn out! I coasted to a stop right in front of Dallas Forbus house on Hwy 280. All the lights were out at the Forbus house so that left out any chance of borrowing their phone to call home. (Yes, it was before the day of cell phones).

Right across the street from the Forbus house was a very old very small country store ran by a man named P.D. Funderburk. I don't recall ever seeing many cars at his store. Mr. Funderburk lived in the rear of the store and he had the reputation of being as mean as a rattle snake! I heard that he was at one time the Grand-Poo-Pah of the local Klan. I also heard that he had even shot at one of his neighbors over some trivial matter. A man not to be trifled with.

Well, here I was in total darkness. It was about ten minutes before 10:00 pm. I knew that I could walk on home and if I were five minutes late I could explain to Daddy why I was late. I'm sure he would understand as I wouldn't mention the burnout! However with "Blood Feast" still on my mind I reluctantly decided to start walking. Just as I reached for the door handle a light came on in Mr. Funderburk's store! I froze! I saw a silhouetted figure in the light of that store that was slightly humped over and I swear that the silhouette had a long knife in his hand! Just like in the "Blood Feast" movie! By this time, I was shaking like a dog trying to pass a peach pit. I locked the doors and lay down in the seat and didn't make a move. I was scared to death.

About 10:20, I saw some headlights coming over the hill. It was the first headlights I had seen since I ran out of gas. Those headlights belonged to my Daddy. I was late and he was out looking for his boy. I always thought my parents were a bit strict on me, however on this one night, I was so glad to see that old red 1956 Ford pickup pull up to where I was stranded. Daddy asked me what had happened. I told him that I was running a bit late and had ran out of gas. I told him that I was just about to get out and walk on home when he came upon me. I apologized for being late and not paying attention to my gas gauge. I couldn't tell him that I was scared to death or about the burnout. After all, I was sixteen years old and a grown man! I had nightmares about that movie and Old Man Funderburk for a very long time after that adventure. RD

Tree Climbing Snake.

Mr Charlie Buzbee had hired three young men, Charles Luker, Ken Saxon and myself to do road work for the county. He was at the time one of the county commissioners. The best I remember he introduced us to a man that he said would oversee us each day. This old man was well past retirement age. His face was a mask of wrinkles and it seemed that each wrinkle could tell a story of a life that had not been very easy. Mr. Buzbee said boys meet 'Pussy'. I think I remember a story about a house full of cats and thus the nickname. Henceforth, I shall simply call him the old man.

The old man took us under his wing and began to teach us the ropes. As I said before he was old and could not move very fast. He had trouble with his joints, feet and legs. If I ever knew his real name I have long since forgotten it but most importantly I remember the old man himself. Boys will be boys and those other two boys or should I call them devils began to play pranks on the old man. Of course I always tried to stop all their pranks. It sure is hard to type with my fingers crossed! The old man would lose the truck keys, his lunch would go missing, etc. He had a habit of taking a nap every day on our lunch break. I still don't know how his boot laces got tied together while he slept that one time! It must have been the devil.

There was one thing the old man was fast at and that was eating. I believe he could eat a whole hamburger in two bites as this allowed for a longer nap. This one day we were working on little New York road and it was time for lunch. No pranks had been played and thus the old man was on guard. We all grabbed our brown bag lunch and began to eat. The old man had found a small tree about fifteen feet high and was reclined against it. His lunch was gone and he was fast asleep. We three stooges were still eating when suddenly we see a big old black snake up in the tree the old man was leaning against. The snake was slowing making its way down the tree.

We became excited and began to shout at the old man to get up. We reported that the snake was climbing down toward him. He opened his eyes and said, "I've lived in Alabama all my life and have never seen a tree climbing snake. Go prank someone else". We assured him that this was no prank but he still did not believe. Ken picks up a big ole limb and tells the old man he is going to hit the snake. I heard the old man say, "Hit him and I'll catch him!"

He proved true to his word. That ole black snake, about five feet long, fell directly in his lap. The snake was flopping around like a chicken with its head cut off and you will never guess what happened next! It renewed his faith!

Scripture tells us that when the Spirit of the Lord gets into us "they shall speak with new tongues." (Mark 16:17). Well the old man called out the name of the Lord and began to speak words I had never heard before. However it's sad to say he lost his renewed faith faster than he had found it. The following scripture says, "They shall take up serpents. . .it shall not hurt them." (Mark 16:18) But the old man cast down that ole snake and when he did there was something inside me that was renewed. My belief in the healing power of snake oil. Some of that ole snake oil must have rubbed off on him because those old feet, legs and joints received new life. That old man moved with the speed of an Olympic sprinter and he tried to kill the snake with heel dust.

Charles and I often speak of that one month from the summer of 1965. If only we could go back for one hour. However the moving finger writes and having written moves on! Ken and the old man have moved on as well but I can still see Ken when he laughs and I can still see that smile on his face wider than the state of Texas. I can hear the old man as he would scold us three but we always knew his bark was worse than his bite. Yes they have gone on and Charles and I are biding our time. I believe that when we enter the gates of Heaven, maybe just maybe, Ken and the old man will be there to greet us. Ken will put his arms around us and say, "Hey, I've got a good one to prank on the old man." The old man will reply, "Not this time boys, not up here."

I believe Jesus enjoys when we laugh at one another, with one another and he loves it when we are able to laugh at ourselves. There will be lots of laughter and joy in heaven. If you don't know Jesus as Lord and Savior don't wait until tomorrow. Tomorrow is not promised ! I believe Ken would say the same ! God Bless! JL

James Kenneth Saxon, age 42, died August 1990 and is buried at Hillview Memorial Park in Alexander City.

The Hams

This incident happened in 1979 during my first year as Tax Assessor for Coosa County and it has to do with the man I called Bart in the Clyde Worthy liquor making and buzzard eating story. One winter day I had to be in the Weogufka area of the county and as I was stopped at the four-way stop in town I heard my named being hollered out. It was Bart standing in front of the post office and he was beckoning me to come over to where he was and I did. Bart thought the world of me and I liked Bart as well. He opened the door and informed me that he had something he wanted to give me and it was really good. At first I thought it was a bottle of moonshine but he said he didn't have the gift with him and I would need to take him home to get it!

Well, he lived about nine miles out of Weogufka and would need a ride to get there. I did not blame him for that. When I pulled up in his yard he invited me into his house and led me to a back room that had some pork shoulders and hams. He had been curing them and they were hanging on a steel wire that he had nailed to the walls. On the floor was discarded newspapers with rats scurrying back and forth on the floor. Bart announced "Luker, I want you to have two of these shoulders as you have always been good to me and I thank you for that." I told Bart that he didn't owe me anything for my friendship and that he didn't need to give me any pork shoulders. After thoroughly explaining to me why he wanted to give them to me I agreed and thanked him.

Immediately he reached to the floor and picked up some of those dirty newspapers and wrapped two shoulders in the paper and carried them and placed them in the trunk of my car. I thanked him several times and left his house for Rockford wondering what I was going to do with those things! As I was walking in the back door of the Courthouse Probate Judge Jasper Fielding was walking out of his office and I told him I was glad to see him as one of his best friends had sent him two salt cured shoulders. He was glad to hear that as he liked cured shoulders and wanted to know who had sent them. I told him that was part of the deal that the one that sent them didn't want him to know who it was until he had eaten both of them. He agreed and I transferred the shoulders to his trunk and he carried them straight home!

About a week later he wanted to know where the shoulders had come from as he had tried to eat them but they were as tough as hickory and as salty as the ocean. I informed him that our mutual friend Bart had given them to me. However I knew of your affection for cured shoulders so I wanted you to have them! He threw the rest of it away and never again accepted a gift from me. CL

Old country boys will give you the shirt off their back! However, you may want to wash it first before you wear it!

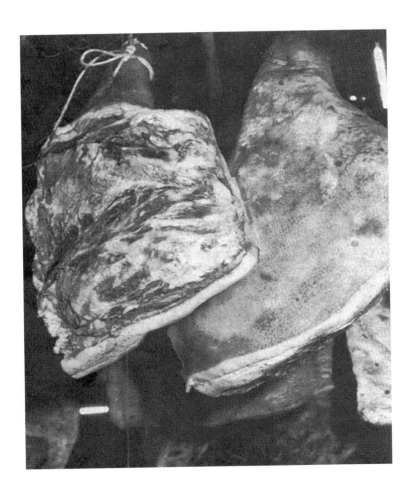

Restrictor Plates – NASCAR ain't got nuttin' on my Daddy

A restrictor plate is simply a plate that is placed between the carburetor and the intake manifold. The diameter of the holes in the restrictor plate are smaller in diameter than that of the intake manifold. This limits the amount of air that can enter the engine. If you limit the amount of air, you limit the amount of fuel and thus you can limit the speed of the vehicle. NASCAR began using these on a limited basis in 1970 and are now required for safety reasons at Daytona and Talladega.

My first real car was a 1954 Chevrolet. It had a 235 cubic inch six cylinder engine with a single barrel Rochester carburetor. That thing had pretty good power for a six cylinder. It was 'Pueblo Tan' with a white top. I think Chevrolet only offered Pueblo Tan on the 1954 model. The reason being it was a butt ugly color. It wasn't tan at all. It reminded you of the inside of a baby diaper after the kid had been eating some of that mushed up carrots and sweet potato baby food!

I was still sweet sixteen in early 1964 and my introduction to restrictor plates had absolutely nothing to do with NASCAR. Seems like the local bank president in Goodwater had called my Daddy and asked, "Bob, do you still have that ugly brown Chevrolet"? Daddy said, "Yes, my son is driving it. Why do you ask?" The Dudley-Do-Right bank president informed Daddy that one day during the previous week he was running late for a meeting in Alexander City. He said that he was driving about seventy mph on Washington Street (a four lane) in an effort to get to the meeting. He said that a young fellow in a brown Chevy like that one had passed him like he was standing still and went completely out of sight in a very short time.

Well when Daddy got off the phone he walked straight to my car, raised the hood and began loosening the nuts on the carburetor. That carburetor was held to the manifold with two nuts. They required a 9/16 inch wrench to remove them. Now in those days Daddy sold Quaker State motor oil. It came in a quart can and the entire can was made of thin metal. He got a pair of tin snips and began cutting the bottom out of one of those empty oil cans. With the tin-snips he shaped it to the same form of the intake manifold and cut two slots in each side in order to be able to slide the plate in and out between the carburetor and manifold. Then he drilled a small hole in the center of that plate. He slid it into place, tightened the nuts, closed the hood and drove off.

A few minutes later he came back. He took the plate out and enlarged the hole in it slightly and then left again. It took several tries but after adjusting the size of the hole in that plate and test driving it about four times he looked at me and said, "Well, I guess that will slow you down".

That old 1954 Chevy would only run fifty-four mph up hill. It would run fifty-four mph down hill! It didn't matter how hard you pressed on the gas pedal fifty-four mph was top speed. It still used the same amount of fuel but it just wasn't gonna go like I wanted it to. You mashed the gas and it didn't go any faster, just made more noise!

I was desperate! What could I do? I went to the parts house and bought myself a brand new 9/16 inch wrench and I hid it under the driver's seat of my car. When I would get about a mile from the house, I would pull over, loosen those two nuts, pull that plate out, tighten the nuts back down and I was clear to fly once again. Of course, before I returned home I had to replace that restrictor plate because Daddy checked it quite often.

I can't tell you how many times I removed and replaced that plate on the side of the road in the middle of the night with no flashlight. I could do it blindfolded. My fingertips still don't have all the feeling in them today because I burned my fingers every time I would grab that carburetor and restrictor plate.

I eventually got busted because I was running late in getting home one Friday night. My weekend curfew was 10:30 pm. That didn't mean 10:35 or 10:36 it meant 10:30! Since I was running late I decided that I didn't have time to replace the restrictor plate. I figured I could sneak around and do it early Saturday morning. Wrong! Daddy got in my car about seven Saturday morning and went for a ride. I was busted! What can I say?

He never replaced that restrictor plate. I guess he knew it was a futile effort. Finally after threats of taking my car away, being grounded for life and the possibility of being sentenced to twenty years in the electric chair I saw the error of my ways. I knew that I had to do things differently. My solution was simply to be more aware of who might be watching me as I continued in my quest for speed! RD

Bethy Trout, Robert's cousin relates a somewhat similar experience with restrictor plates. This is her story. I feel your pain, cousin!

My Daddy must have done the same thing to the 1953 Pontiac Chieftain we had. The only difference is he didn't tell me about it! He did this to slow down my oldest sister's land speed record attempts between Alex City and Goodwater. His uninformed restricting nearly cost me and the Chieftain right near the bridge just south of Paul's shop on present day highway nine. I had intrepidly punched it to pass another vehicle on the straightaway and lo and behold another car was rapidly coming towards me from the other direction! I floor boarded the formerly responsive beast and nothing!

I'll never forget the look of absolute fear the gentleman in the other car had on his face as he swerved off the road to let me continue my course! Still in a state of shock I drove straight to my Dad's shop to inform him there was something seriously wrong with the two-toned green two door! He then told me he had put a 'governor' on the carburetor! What? It slowed me down alright. It almost got me killed. Wish I'd known about the 9/16 inch wrench!

Me, my wayward cousin Tommy and the '54 in the background!

Random Thoughts

As I was grilling this afternoon and talking to my son in the Outer Banks, NC I had a strong remembrance of my youth and our exciting times in Goodwater, Alabama. I do remember that people did not go out to eat much. There weren't many places to go! Plus money was scarce most times. In Goodwater we had the Old Hickory, Pan-AM Cafe and later the Dairy Delite. If you really wanted to go out to eat you would go to Alex City to the Quail Restaurant, Lake Hill, BonFire or the Airport Cafe. We always went to the Airport Cafe as they had good Bar-B-Q. They had a swimming pool, too! To get your order they offered curb service. A young lady would come to your car and you gave them the order of what you desired to have. What I remember most was that when they brought you your order you got an aluminum tray that attached to the car window, if it was rolled up a few inches and the Coca Colas were in glass six ounces bottles. Obviously, that was before the bigger bottles came out.

We were more concerned about the city name on the bottom of the Coke bottle than the taste. Did they even have French Fries then? All I remember was potato chips. I do remember the cost for a family of five was usually less than $5.00. They did serve you if you were without a shirt or shoes. Boys just didn't wear all of that in the summer except for church! We wore bow ties to church at that time. Every Sunday you wore the same pants, shirt, Sunday shoes and bow tie. Never a question or a doubt about that.

If you had money and gas you could always go to Kowliga Beach. We usually went there on the Fourth of July! Not to the restaurant but to the beach. As you may remember Kowliga Beach was on the other side of the lake from the restaurant. The water was so clean and clear. They had picnic tables for first come first serve for free. What a time. I remember the "Are you ready ski daddy!" ads. Most all boats were outboards with thirty-five horsepower motors and made of wood. Fred Brooks related how he learned to ski behind a Johnson twenty-five horse that must have weighed 500lbs on the back of a sky blue wooden sixteen footer. It took forever for it to plane and get up to speed so his Dad put about 8-10 concrete blocks in the front which were padded with beach towels so they wouldn't beat the bottom out. It helped some but the boat still took quite a beating. Glory Days!!!!! CL

Halloween Doings

Tommy Dark tells about an episode he claims not to remember but that a classmate told him recently that had occurred. The classmate says Tommy was heavily involved. Here is Tommy's version of the story. I don't remember any of it and think I may be getting set up as a scapegoat in this sordid incident! Being the angelic son that my mother had prayed for I have serious doubts that I was even remotely involved. I shall relate the story as it was told to me.

We were doing our thing on Halloween getting into all sorts of mischief. I guess we learned from the older students at Goodwater High School and had to follow the tradition. Then again we may have started the tradition ourselves. At any rate the plan was to get on top of all those downtown building on Halloween night and toss M-80s down on the street. We planned to throw some close to the police station and then take off running!

According to my classmate's account I scaled the row of buildings and got on the roofs close to Luker's Truck and Tractor. After a few minutes on top I supposedly fell through one of those roofs and to the floor I went. They all helped me back after I found an old table to stand on. That's what he told me anyway.

He swore this happened but that was over fifty years ago and my mind sometimes goes blank. I will state for the record that I do not believe I would have embarked on such a dastardly deed. I got blamed for many things I didn't do so I will just say maybe it happened. Rumors are that it was probably Pattie Lee's dad's place as she told me a while back her dad's store developed a water leak about that time. I am reasonably sure it was probably my evil cousin Robert Dark instead of me. I usually took the rap for most of his shenanigans!

I did attempt to toss a firecracker out of the back window of a friends car when I was in high school. I think I was in the back seat of Walt Dowdle's red 1955 Chevy the night I threw the firecracker and the window was up. It just happened the car was exactly in front of the police station. Nobody in the car knew I was planning on doing it. It was a failure as the window was up. The person had just washed his car and windows. I think I got yelled at but in the end we all laughed after we got our hearing back!

Robert Dark however swears it was not him. He claims he never hung around with hooligans. He states he does not recall that event but someone did throw an M-80 in the front door of the police station from a building across the street while poor Charlie Levi was taking a nap inside at the time! Also there were a few times that boys had been known to throw several bales of hay on the bridge and set them on fire.

Curtis Dawkins can verify some of that mischief. Since we are talking Halloween here is my fondest memory in Goodwater in 1968 I think. We were all hanging out at the Dairy Delite (owned by Mr. McBried at the time) when Kenneth Ledbetter and some others thought it would be cute to fill a tire with diesel fuel and light it. They rolled it down the hill beside the nursing home and it ended up hitting J. B. Kelly's house and fire was everywhere. J. B. came outside in pajamas with a shotgun. No damage was done and nobody was hurt thank God. We took off running!

Charles Luker recalls some Halloween antics this way! The teenagers got on top of Mr. W.M. Pruet's store as it was easy access and threw cherry bombs at the police department. I remember one night the barrage was taking place and the police ran to his car and opened the door such that he could apprehend the outlaws! In the three seconds his door was opened a lucky throw landed a cherry bomb inside the police car. Needless to say when it exploded the police evacuated the car. I believe we called him Pop McCrary and he was from Rockford. We would go see him and he would tell us how tough he was! Not so much that night though!

I remember when Chief Homer Smith lived in the old Billy and Judy Phillips house next to Dr. McClendon's house and always like to tell us boys how tough he had been and was. Halloween we devised a bomb of a Vienna sausage can and about seven or eight cherry bombs inside the can taped tightly with duct tape with one fuse sticking out. Needless to say when it went off it was rather dramatic. As the culprits rounded the corner at Luker's Tractor they could hear bird shot hitting the store! It wouldn't have been so bad if it hadn't been on his porch! I believe he called them something and it was not nice! At least that the way I heard it!

Also there was the incident with the Goodwater Police Department and their 1963 green Chevrolet that went missing! It wasn't really missing. Some boys had pushed it behind the police department where the jail was and locked it!

There was twenty-three sets of keys for the car but they were all on the same chain and it mysteriously went missing also! It took several days before access to the car was regained. Mayor A.O. Holmes was not pleased!

Speaking of the Jail

Sometime during the early 1960's a Northerner was visiting some relatives in Goodwater. At some point during his stay he apparently was involved in a fracas at the 'Dew Drop Inn'! This led to his being taken into custody by the local law enforcement officials and placed in the Goodwater jail. Apparently he felt that his civil rights were somehow violated during his incarceration process and had filed a complaint with some office of the Federal Gubmint upon his return to the nawth.

A couple of months later two men in dark suits showed up at my Dad's shop. They informed my Dad that they had been assigned the task of investigating the 'incident'. My Dad told them that he had not witnessed the individual being placed into the jail, but that one of his employees, Henry, had told him about seeing the police trying to lock him up.

They interviewed Henry and his comments were something like the following, "I done seen it! He was mad as a wet hen! Ebery time they tried to throw him in the jail, he would bounce wight back out wike a wubba ball!"

After the interview, the agents told my Dad that after interviewing Henry, they now had a better understanding of what had happened. I think the case was then officially closed.

That alley way to the jail between Holmes Drug Store, my Dad's shop and the Police station saw a lot of traffic in those days. I saw some things that were both comical and sad. That jail house is still there but not used any more!

In those days, there was not much crime in Goodwater. I never recall seeing anyone being locked up that wasn't under the influence. It was a two cell jail and had no heat and certainly no air conditioning only a couple of open bar windows. I think it was really built to accommodate Percy Glenn. RD

Charles Luker says Percy Glenn started so many fires in that old jail they finally quit locking him up with matches in his pocket! Curtis Dawkins says his Uncle Lester Smith spent many nights in that jail as he was one of the town's drunks!

All Day Singings

There were few things bigger in my youth than an All Day Singing. Some folks called them Homecomings. Doesn't matter what you called it, it was a big deal. Only thing that compared was a wedding or funeral but they were usually only one time occurrences. The singings came around every year. A singing is when the church holds a service (predetermined date) and usually calls in a guest preacher, one or more singing groups and it, as the name implies, lasts all day.

Seems like it was usually June or July and it was so hot that when the preacher started talking about Hellfire and brimstone you thought you were already halfway there! The ladies were fanning themselves with the hand fans provided by the local funeral home or insurance company. Religious photo on one side, advertisement on the other! Gotta love capitalism! The ladies would congregate in the church and listen to 'The Message' and the singing, the men would gather under various shade trees and swap lies and an occasional sip.

The kids who were lucky enough to escape the church torture played. There was family, cousins we hadn't seen since last years singing and perfect strangers but we all were of the same tribe that day! The girls would form a gaggle and giggle, gossip and flirt with the boys and the boys, depending on their age, would seriously try to ignore them or try to cut one out of the herd and talk her into going out behind the cemetery! We played in the cemetery, in the woods about the area, behind the church and anywhere that suited us.

This was way before flush toilets were common and most of the churches we went to had outhouses. One for the men and another for the ladies. Usually out back and in the edge of the woods. One church we went to had a spring out back where you could get a cool drink of water. The spring had a concrete thingie built around it with a pipe where the spring continuously flowed with cool, clear, clean water from the bowels of the earth. There was a gourd dipper that everybody shared. Not very sanitary I guess but what did we know?!

The highlight was the dinner. For those raised up north dinner is the noon meal, supper the evening one, we do NOT do lunch! All these little blue haired ladies would spend days cooking, canning, salting and making all manner of eats. They always brought their best. And I do mean best. Tables that seemed like they stretched for miles groaned with all manner of meats, casseroles, pies, cakes and you name it, it was there.

Fried, baked, boiled, raw, etc. Sweet tea, Kool-aid, lemonade, etc. Reminds me of the old rhyme that goes, "I wish I were rubber skinned, instead of steel and tight, so I could eat a thousand things, so I could eat all night!" Believe me I tried. My Grannie's specialty was fried apple pies, but that's another story. As it started to approach noon we would start circling the tables trying to scope out where the best stuff was so we could be sure to go there first and get some before it was all gone. There was an art to it that has probably faded away by now. Load up your plate and find a spot under one of the trees or a pickup tailgate or whatever was available and eat. Repeat until you couldn't do it anymore. After the initial melee we would go around and make another plate to take home. This would be our supper. That is if it made it home!

My grannie made fried apple pies. Not just any ole fried pie but one that was worthy of taking to homecoming! For those who may not know it is kinda like an apple turnover but that does not even do it justice. As the name implies they were fried. Not in Crisco or any of that other shortening stuff. My grannie used lard. Pure pork lard! It was the secret ingredient. Fried to a golden brown on one side, flipped over and fried on the other. Pure heaven in a skillet.

When we went to homecoming those who knew her knew that she had fried apple pies and would sneak them before the official opening of the meal. A flagrant violation of all know protocols re homecoming! After she died my sisters made some and took them with a note that they were in remembrance of her. They weren't the same! PGG

Dr. Cockerham and Percy

Dr. Cockerham was Goodwater's finest M.D. He was indeed a fine gentleman and physician. Back in the early 1960s, my dad ran a garage in Robert Smith's (Smith Motor Company) building. The back door to that shop faced the police/fire department. There was an alley that was between the police station, Dad's shop and Holmes Drug store. At the end of that alley, attached to the rear of the police station was the city jail. It had one door and as best I can recall had just two cells. There were two barred (window) openings with nothing but bars. There was no glass. Just bars. I could almost write a book on what I have seen take place in that alley and jail.

One particular event even resulted in a 'Federal' investigation (but that's another story). One Saturday afternoon, Sandy Hardeman and Cleburne Ogburn received a call about a cutting incident at the 'Dew Drop Inn'. The Dew Drop was a favorite hang-out of the infamous Percy Glenn. As I walked to the back door of Dad's shop I saw Sandy and Cleburne dragging this fellow down the alley. They stopped just short of the jail and were just outside the back door of the shop. They were holding this fellow down on the ground. (The alley was dirt, no pavement). He had blood all across the lower half of his shirt and was screaming "Somebody help me! I done been cut up!" It was fairly obvious to me, even as a youngster, that he was a little bit impaired by alcohol.

A few minutes later, Dr. Cockerham pulled his white 1957 Ford "Woody" station wagon into the alley. He parked and got out with his little black doctor bag. I feel that it is important to say that Dr. Cockerham told my Dad that when the city called him out for this type of thing they paid him a flat $5.00 per call. While Sandy and Cleburne were holding this guy down on the ground Dr. Cockerham knelt down in the dirt beside him. He opened his little black bag, pulled out some scissors and cut the man's shirt open. He then took out a small bottle of alcohol or something, soaked a piece of gauze with it and wiped it around the cut on the man's stomach. Next he pulled out this little curved needle with some kind of thread on it and began sewing up the cut. The man began screaming at the top of his lungs, "Doc, ya killin' me! Ya gotta give me something!" Dr. Cockerham never missed a stitch! He simply said, "Hell, they didn't give you anything when they cut you did they?"

A few minutes later the Doc was finished and the bad boy was escorted into the jail. Times were a bit different in those days. I have seen many, many things in that alley. RD

Old Percy Glenn was jailed frequently for being intoxicated. Percy was alright though. In later years he had the pleasure of setting the mattress in the jail on fire! I think I told the story about Percy once putting a fox hound out of the owners misery but the dog magically re-appeared. Sheriff Estes had several fox dogs and he was out trying to gather them up and that was when he saw the dog that Percy had supposedly shot or was told to shoot! Percy was at the time a prisoner in the Coosa County Jail. When Mr. Estes and Percy were out looking for the other dogs they rounded a curve and the dog that Mr. Estes had told Percy to kill stood up on the side of the road and the sheriff asked Percy what that was? Percy told the sheriff that it looked like the dog he done kilt! CL

Maybe Percy should have offered the Doc a few bucks for pain killers!

The Jail!

Mr. Wizard saves Mr. Parker

A way back in the early 1960s, Mrs. Parker and her husband lived next door to my Dad's shop. I don't recall ever seeing Mr. Parker but this one time. I think he was in poor health and required the use of oxygen. Mrs. Parker seemed to have the personality of a "Bent Dempsey Dumpster" and the only time I ever saw her was when she was telling on myself and my wayward cousin Tommy Dark for doing something either outside, inside, over or under my Dad's shop.

One day she came running into the shop and told Dad that Mr. Parker was dying because he had run out of oxygen. She was frantic and wanted Dad to call for help. My Dad looked at me and Thomas (Shag) Graham and said, "Get the torch and roll it down to Mrs. Parker's house now!" He grabbed a couple of pairs of pliers and a couple of wrenches and ran ahead of us. I looked at Shag and said, "Did he say get the torch?" Shag said, "Yes sir and I think he wants it now." At this point I thought my Dad had lost his ever loving mind. The torch was a two-wheeled cart that had a bottle of acetylene and a bottle of oxygen, complete with gauges, hoses and various cutting/welding attachments.

Shag and I wrestled the torch cart down some steps to Mrs. Parker's yard and then up her front steps and into the house. I was still confused as I couldn't see how Daddy was going to use that torch to help poor old Mr. Parker. I couldn't imagine how he was gonna 'weld' him back to health!

Then I witnessed some "Dark" magic. My Dad began disconnecting Mr. Parker's empty oxygen bottle hose and sticking the end of the torch into that hose. He then turned on the torch's oxygen valve and in just a minute or two Mr. Parker began breathing normal again. Slowly he regained a little color in his face. I believe he was very close to checking out of this old world.

Shag and I were totally amazed at this and there is no doubt that my Dad's quick thinking saved Mr. Parker that day. We left the torch there until an ambulance arrived with a new bottle of oxygen for Mr. Parker. Those folks have long since gone to another place and the house is no longer there but I can close my eyes and see it as if it were yesterday. Small town redneck engineering at it's best! RD

Valentines

Back in the day (that's what old people are wont to say when they're gonna talk about a time long gone) we used to give out Valentines to each other in school. There was an unwritten rule that you had to give everybody one so that no one felt left out. This was not a government mandate or anything, just kids realizing that if someone didn't get cards they would feel bad and we didn't want that. You might not like the person or she might be the ugliest girl in the third grade (also known as a virgin) but that was no excuse to be mean. Boys gave boys cards as did girls to girls. There was no sexual connotation to it as there seems to be today. Just be my friend and I'll be yours. Simpler times.

Most cards were purchased in packages from the local drug store, grocery or curb market. Some were more artistic and designed and drew their own cards. These were usually from someone that wanted to impress you or were too poor to buy any. My friend Bruce comes to mind but that's another story. Anyway, we would get a paper sack and decorate it with crayon drawings and hearts and put our name on it and tape it to the back of our desk. This was usually about a week or so before Valentine's day so there was plenty of time to drop in the cards.

It was a major faux pas to be caught putting a card in someones bag. Secrecy and such. Minor league James Bonds we were! Some folks signed their cards while others expounded on the mystery by signing as a secret admirer or some such! We were not supposed to look at the cards until Valentine's Day but sometimes the temptation was just too great and we would sneak a peek. Looking for that one from that special person that you hoped would give you that 'extra special' card that showed that you were 'The One'! Some folks even went whole hog and added candy or a sucker or some other treat to their card. A wonderful delight indeed! Candy hearts with a message on them were the rage. I believe they are still sold to this day. I can only imagine one with a message like 'I twerk for you'! Wish I had kept some of those old cards! PGG

Cleaning the Gym

Scott Rogers and I were in the 10th grade and we developed a method and a secret to cleaning the nasty floor in the old gym that was really admired by Coachs Gene and James Hayes. We had done such a good job that we got out of Mrs. Jesse Robbins study hall frequently to clean the floor especially for home basketball games. It was a really simple process! I would take a couple of two liter coke containers and walk in front of the dust mop as Scotty pushed the mop and I would sprinkle water out of the bottles in front of the mop! It looked as if it had been waxed. The first time Coach Gene saw it he came up with that red faced smile and wanted to know what we had done? I laughed and told him I would never tell!

Anyway, Coach James wrote an excuse one day for Scotty, Larry Shivers and I to go to the gym to work on the floor. Larry wasn't going to the gym but had another daily task to do for Coach Hayes. In Coach's excuse he said today and everyday and had our names listed below. He underlined Larry Shivers and everyday in the excuse meaning he wanted Larry excused everyday. We simply corrected that mistake by underlining our names too! It worked. We never went back to study hall as we goofed off somewhere. Mr. Westbrook would let us drive to the post office in his red pickup to get the mail. Of course we investigated a lot of places in our trips to the Post Office. Coach James always signed his excuse JCH and I could copy it to perfection. On several occasions when someone needed an excuse Coach would tell them to get Old Charlie Boy to sign it as they might not recognise his own signature! CL

Basketball Games, Playing and Refereeing

The most amazing basketball game I have ever played in. It happened in 1964 and we were playing the Weogufka Pirates for the first game of the season. I did not play well enough to play on the "A" team so I played the "B" Team. I had more fun anyway. We usually had our first basketball game just a few days after football season and we had not yet adjusted to not tackling our opponents. In a small high school most all the boys played all of the sports like football, basketball, baseball, shooting marbles and shooting dice. High dice only. No craps as we were not as smart as Tommy Dark! Anyway, we were beating Weogufka fairly easily until the football mentality came back.

Also, a new rule was added that year as you had to raise your hand if a foul was called on you or the referee would call a technical foul on you. I had two fouls in the first minute plus two technical fouls! I kindly ask Charlie Brown, a referee, what in the world was the technical foul for and he said, "Open that mouth once more and you will get another technical!" I looked at Coach Gene Hayes and he told me he had forgotten to inform us to raise our hands when a foul was called.

The next down time the court I was passing the ball to someone and it slipped out of my hand and hit Charlie Brown right between the eyes. He didn't think that was near as funny as I did but it was sort of an accident. As the game progressed we started losing players for having five fouls. Well we were down to four players and we were holding on to our slim lead as five against four ain't hardly fair! When the final buzzer sounded, the game was over, the score was tied and we had three players left for overtime. Al Westbrook, Bobby Smith and yours truly. Well, we were doing well just to stay up with them but the tide changed when Bobby got a rebound under the Weogufka goal and wanting to make two points he shoots it right back in for two points! For them! As we were carrying the ball down the court Gene Hayes hollered to Bobby and told him, "That's the way to go! If you can't beat them just join them!" Well, anyway I fouled out in another minute or so and on my last foul Charlie Brown called it and pointed to the door. I gave him a proper salute for a job well done. The gym was crowded as we were playing in their auditorium and as I passed through the door I gave some smart a$$ remark and the men in Weogufka just hollered. We lost! But, we all had fun. Their gym was really small but at least the roof didn't leak! CL

J.T. McDonald relates the following. I had a game at Weogufka one year as a "B" team that I will never forget. I was on fire that night and could not miss. I was so pumped up and too aggressive. I guess you would say I was a little out of control. I fouled out in the second quarter before halftime! I went up to block a shot by Houston Varner and the ref blew the whistle. My fifth personal foul so I was outta there. The referee was Johnny Newberry who later became my mentor, my fellow official and most of all my friend. He and I called a lot of games together over the years.

He passed away at age 56. I was 46 at the time and now some twenty years later I am still carrying on that striped-shirt tradition! He was one of the best men I ever knew! Rest in peace, Johnny, no foul!

Charles agreed Johnny was a really good man and referee and I enjoyed working games with him. I called several games with Charlie Brown and he was a sight. Every time Charlie called a game the folks wanted to whip him and a few did. Charlie and I called a game in the Hackneyville Invitation once. The game was between New Site and Daviston. It was really close and a good ballgame but someone got after Charlie after the game. The next night when I went to call a game Mr. Pat King and Mr. Welch, the principal, met me at the door and ushered me into the office. They were looking a little pale. Once in the office they asked me if I had had any trouble last night with any of the fans and I told them everyone was really nice to me and I had no problems. Then they told me that Charlie Brown had a confrontation with some folks and there was some pushing and shoving and they were afraid that I had been confronted also. I have seen Charlie Brown running down the court calling a foul hitting the floor on his knees and slide all the way under the goal. He did that once or twice to me and I had to laugh at his antics!

I remember the first and only time I played a basketball game in Equality and it equated to sleeping in a VW. Goodwater had the better team but I think we lost to them. The ceiling was about twelve feet high and the goal was ten feet! Every time we would shoot we would hit the ceiling and it was called a dead ball and went to your opponent. They probably didn't want us to come back because they spent most of the night replacing shattered 200 watt light bulbs that we broke! They had a really good player in Jerry Fuller and he had a jump shot that never got over eleven feet high and he stripped the net every time he shot. Heck, we couldn't even shoot a free shot without hitting the ceiling. Their court was rather short but that was not the problem. The height was the problem. Of course we liked to run a fast break on a missed opponents shot. It was somewhat subdued by the length but still the pass for a fast break would hit the ceiling. The end lines for the court was the wall and the stage and it usually resulted in an abrupt stop! But, we all had a good time and the memories last! I believe Jasper Fielding was their coach, principal and teacher and I think he ran the concession stand too!

I went to Bibb Graves High School in Millerville, Alabama to call a couple of games one night. Bibb Graves always had a really good team and great coaches. The coach then was Frank Toland and Frank and I had had several classes together at Auburn and we played golf together a good bit. Frank was a rather unique fellow as he didn't show a lot of emotion, good or bad, during a ballgame. He was intense and expected his players to play as coached and the officials to do a fair job of calling the game. There is one thing an official never does and that is when you make a bad call look at the coach! Yes, I made my share of bad calls. Charging and blocking fouls are somewhat judgmental and the coach whose player it is called on usually has a lot to say. One of the advantages of not hearing well! I called a blocking foul on a Millerville player right in front of where the Millerville team and Coach Toland was sitting. Frank never hollered at the officials and he knew I wasn't going to look at him. When I called this foul his response was, "Hey! Ref! Look at me!" I had to steal a glance and he was just looking at me and shaking his head. If he had seen me laughing going back down the court he would have been mad. Frank Toland was a special coach and is a special person. He always displayed class. He was a great high school player, college classmate and a great coach that set a great example for his players.

I had to go to Ranburne High School one night to call two games and it was quiet a trip from Goodwater. Ranburne is in Randolph or Cleburne County and is on the Georgia Line. One end line was about six inches from a concrete brick wall. They even had a dashed line for an inbound pass. I was back peddling on a fast break and forget about the wall. When I hit, it felt like the wall moved a foot and I had stuck to it! It didn't knock me out but we had to stop the game for a few minutes until I recovered from the shock and to change my pants. I didn't really have to change my pants. The other official that I didn't really know that well offered a lot of good insight after that by telling me I needed to be careful as there was a wall close to that endline! I thanked him for his brilliant observation and he looked dumbfounded! I never went back over there again. CL

How I Failed Miserably at Becoming a Millionaire'!

At some point during the early 1980s I finally realized that I was not going to win the Publisher's Clearing House grand prize. Although I had entered their contests for years and had magazines arriving daily it became apparent that it was just not gonna happen! That's when I decided that I had to take matters into my own hands. I would write a book and sell it to the masses. I would be rich and famous. (Well, it was not actually a book but more of an informational pamphlet of some thirty or so typewritten pages.)

The 'book' was directed toward the general population on how to ensure quality collision repairs on vehicles that incorporated the relatively new 'Uni-Body' designs and covered the theory behind the 'McPherson strut' style system of steering and suspension. It also covered the general repair procedures when dealing with welding and straightening techniques of the new high strength steels and the designed crush zones used in these vehicles. Cars were fast becoming 'frame free'. Without boring my readers with all the details, suffice it to say that during that time period, there were many repairs being performed across America that were just plumb dangerous. I alone was going to save the world though information and was convinced that millions would be clamoring to purchase my informational package.

I had five hundred copies of my, soon to be famous, publication printed. I advertised in *Popular Mechanics, Popular Science* and the *Grit* newspaper. I ran these ads in the back section of each publication for three months. (You know those tiny little three or four line ads that promised everything under the sun!) My informational packet sold for less than $10.00 and after a year, I had sold an amazing five copies all across America. I ended up throwing the other 495 copies in the trash and simply marked it off as a learning experience. All is not lost, however, as there are five people out there who are ahead of the game by purchasing my life changing product.

Apparently, I was ahead of my time and America just wasn't ready to accept the vast information from someone like me who was definitely 'A-Legend-In-My-Own-Mind'. I have not given up on becoming a millionaire. A fellow told me once that the only way to become a millionaire was to owe a million dollars. I took his advice and although I'm not quite there yet, give me another week or two!
RD

Mellow Yellow

Growing up just to the left of the middle of nowhere I was pretty much insulated from the so-called drug culture of the day or as they called it the Sixties! We would occasionally see something about it on the nightly news or it might get mentioned on the radio. Seems there was a lot of it going on at colleges and in San Francisco which might as well have been a million miles away. Some of the songs at that time were somewhat positive about the use of drugs and peace, love, dove if you will. Well that thing about the free love kinda got my attention as I would occasionally have strange urges and twinges here and there. So being the great intellect I was back then and most of the songs equated drug use with free love I figured if I could just get hooked up with the drugs the free love would follow!

Well there were no drugs to be had anywhere in the area except for moonshine and the songs didn't mention that at all. A few country songs did but there was no free love in those so the 'shine was right out! Now if I could get some seeds I could be like Jim Stafford and the song "Wildwood Weed" but there was no way to order them at the time and as I said there was not a weed, at least a smokable one, this side of San Fran! What was a poor country boy to do?!

Somewhere along about this time Donovan came out with a song called "Mellow Yellow". It included a lyric about an electrical banana and it was highly rumored at the time that the song was about getting high by smoking dried banana peels. At last, a break! I could get banana peels and the free love was soon to follow. Never mind that there were no girls within a few miles of where we lived but they would find their way to me. I was set.

Grannie would occasionally buy bananas and the next time she did I discretely took the peels and placed them outside to dry. I had to be careful about their placement to preclude any questions along the line of "What the He. . . uh. . . heck are you doing?"

Being the double naught spy that I was I placed them on the roof just above the steps to the porch. I could easily reach them but they could not be seen. I bided my time. Seems like it took forever for the peels to dry. Finally the big day came. The peels were dry.

I went up to the old barn and carefully chopped up the peels and rolled them in some cigarette papers I got from Grandpa. He smoked Prince Albert in the can and I had learned to roll cigarettes by rolling some for him as he got older. I vacillated between smoking them naked or clothed what with the free love thing to come along any minute. I kept my clothes on as I figured that undressing was what was considered foreplay, at least that is what I had heard at school from some of the older guys! So I roll up the peels and lit one of those bad boys up. It was nasty. Now I had smoked some pretty bad things up till then such as rabbit tobacco wrapped in a piece of a brown paper grocery bag. It wasn't too bad. I bought a fifty cent foot long cigar at a souvenir shop once and tried to smoke it. It wasn't too bad. This was bad! Not only that it did not in any way get me high! Plus the women never showed up! I'm still waiting on that free love thing! PGG

Familiarity Breeds Contempt

I started my teaching career in the Fall of 1974 and I'll admit that I was as lost as an inebriated flea on a hairy ape's butt. I remember standing in front of my first class of around twenty young people. I stammered and sputtered and told them everything I knew during the first fifteen minutes of class. It was indeed a frightening experience because I had no idea of how or what I could offer these young people for the remainder of that class much less the entire school year. I was indeed in panic mode.

After that first day, I had a long talk with my Dad. I told him that I didn't think I could be a teacher. He laughed at my first day jitters and we had a long conversation on what I might be faced with on a day-to-day basis in the classroom. One thing in particular that he shared with me was, "Always remember, familiarity breeds contempt". I didn't understand that at first but he told me that I had made the decision to be a teacher of others. He said that not only did I have a duty to impart what little technical knowledge I possessed but to also assist in how these young people would live their lives long after they left my classroom. He said, "You cannot teach them to respect you as an individual, as that respect is earned, but you can demand that they show respect to your position as an instructor during their short visit with you."

He told me to always draw a communication line between student and teacher. This "Line in the Sand" included never allowing a student to call me by my first name. He said that, "To your students, regardless of their age, you should always be addressed as Mr. Dark". I followed his advice for over thirty-two years and during those years I returned that respect by calling my students Mr. or Ms. Smith, Johnson or whatever.

Now I shared this seemingly useless bit of information to convey an incident that happened back in the early 1980s that involved a student from another class (not mine). There was a retired Army Major, several years older than me, that was using his VA benefits to further his education. He would occasionally walk through my shop and in front of all my students would yell out "Hey Robbie, how is it going?" or "What's up Robbie?".

My students would look at me with this look of "Is that guy your best friend?" One day he walked through the shop and yelled, "Hey Robbie, how is it going?" I called his hand and did so in front of all my students!

I said, "Mr. Smith, my name is not 'Robbie' but if you need to address me in the future please feel free to call me what my parents, my wife and all my friends call me." He said, "Oh, OK, sure, what do they call you?" I said, "They call me Mr. Dark!" That quickly put an end to his shenanigans.

How many of you can ever recall addressing a teacher by his or her first name? It was all about respect. Not about respecting me as an individual but about respecting the position of an individual who was only trying to make a life better for others. I cannot remember one teacher in my life's journey that I ever addressed other than Mr. or Mrs. Recently, I talked to one of my former students from the Mid-80s. He kept addressing me as "Mr. Dark". I told him that my name was "Robert". He said, "You have always been Mr. Dark and you will always be Mr. Dark." He also thanked me for helping to assist him in his thoughts and outlook on life. I may get all kinds of negative responses from this story, but I think my Dad nailed it. What does 'respect' mean to our young people today? Good question. RD

Goodwater Goes Global

The powers that be, for some reason, decided to have our Squadron's annual Christmas get-together at a traditional Japanese restaurant in downtown Kokura, Japan. This was 1967 and a long way from Goodwater and what this old country boy was used to. This was the kind of place that you had to take your shoes off before entering. The floors were covered in bamboo mats and the tables were only about eighteen inches tall.

We sat on the floor around those tables "Indian Style". The waitresses were what I would call "Geisha Girls". They had their faces painted white, hair all done up on top of their head and wore Kimonos (you know, those floor length towel looking things with what looked like a parachute strapped on the back). I never have figured out what that parachute looking thing was for. Now keep in mind that a traditional Geisha trains for years in the art of serving food. I've been told they are pretty good in other services as well although I have no personal knowledge of that.

Once we were all settled into our (uncomfortable) place on the floor around the table, the ladies began bringing out our drinks (Hot Sake), eating utensils (chop sticks), empty bowls and other bowls containing the food. Every movement and every placement of the items on the table seemed to be an exact science. Everything had a place and everyone's items were placed in the exact fashion. I was impressed until they actually started bringing the food out.

Here is a rundown. First they placed some cooked rice in your bowl. Then several pieces of raw fish were placed on that. They followed that up with what looked like cooked turnip greens (turns out it was seaweed). Then came the octopus tentacles cut into about two inch strips (I'm not kidding when I say they still had the little suckers on them). Of course everything was then splattered with a generous helping of soy sauce. Then they came out with a large bowl of eggs still in the shell. My thought was that while I wasn't gonna eat that bowl of nastiness at least I could eat a couple of boiled eggs. Wrong answer!

I was sitting next to the end of the table and the Geisha lady started by cracking a raw egg and letting it slither over my buddy's bowl of horror. When she came to me, I instinctively leaned over my bowl and place my arms over it. I looked up at her and said "Oh hell no. Hold the eggs and bring me some more Sake". I must admit that I ate a little of everything in my bowl. The seaweed tasted like, well, seaweed (hard to explain). The octopus didn't have a bad taste but the more I chewed it the bigger it seemed to get. The raw fish was well a bit raw, but the rice was pretty good. It's hard to mess up rice.

I tried those foods for two reasons. One, I knew that I would probably never again get the opportunity to experience traditional Japanese cuisine and two, if you drink enough hot Sake you will eat just about anything. We ended the meal with several toasts of hot Sake. If you have never tried hot or cold Sake you should try it at least once. If you can't find it just pour yourself up a nice shot glass of kerosene. Would I do it again? I doubt it. I would probably be just as well off eating a road-kill sandwich. RD

The Salt Sandwich

Charles Luker wrote a story that reminds me of something that I will never forget. It happened one Saturday afternoon when I was around ten and my brother Tim was around five years old. Since I was a growing boy, I often got hungry between meals and usually found something to snack on. My folks didn't buy many "store bought" snacks and lunch meat was a luxury! I usually wound up making myself a ketchup and mayonnaise sandwich. I had just finished making my sandwich and Tim walked in and said, "Fix me one". I promptly told the little kid to get lost and that I wasn't making him a sandwich or anything else. My little brother was always cramping my style in those days.

Mama was in another room making something with her sewing machine and poor little Timmy-boy ran to her complaining that I was being mean to him and wouldn't fix him a sandwich. I heard Mama from the other room "Butch, you fix your baby brother a ketchup and mayonnaise sandwich and quit being mean to him". I had not even taken the first bite of my sandwich and now I had to make 'The Baby' one. I was mad as a wet hen particularly after he came running back into the kitchen with that "nana-nana-boo-boo" grin on his face. Well, I spread ketchup on one piece of loaf bread and then mayonnaise on another piece. Finally when Tim wasn't looking I took the top off of the salt-shaker and turned the ketchup side white with salt. I used almost all the salt in the shaker and then put the two halves back together. I'll fix his wagon I thought.

Tim wasn't as stupid as I figured because the first thing he did when I handed him his sandwich was to open it up for an inspection! Bam! He runs off to show Mama what I had done. Mama came into the kitchen holding that sandwich and said, "Give Tim your sandwich! This one is yours and you WILL eat all of it". Well, I had no choice but to eat it. I can still taste it in the back of my mind. It's a taste that never ever quite goes away. Up until that point I really liked ketchup and mayonnaise sandwiches but I don't recall ever having the urge to eat another one since that day! A memory that lingers since somewhere around 1957. Some lessons in life are learned the hard way and the harder they are to learn, the easier it is to remember their cause and effect. This could be why till this day I try to limit my salt intake! RD

Talking to the Lord

One afternoon when I was about thirteen a man came driving up to my Daddy's shop in an old beat up 1950 model Plymouth. He stepped out of the old Plymouth and began walking towards my Daddy and I noticed several things about him. He had on a dark colored suit, white shirt and a what looked like a child's tie. That tie only came down about three buttons past his collar. He had a stomach that hung way over his belt and he could not have buttoned that coat if he tried. There were snuff stains all over that white shirt.

He walked up to Daddy and extended his hand for a handshake. He said, "Good-a morning-a I'm-a Brother Smith-a from up in Talladega County-a". Daddy shook his hand and said, "I'm Bobby Dark. What can I help you with?" That fellow looked at Daddy and said, "Mr. Dark-a, I was-a talking-a to the Lord-a last-a night-a and he told-a me that-a you were-a going to give-a me one hundred-a dollars to help-a build-a my new church-a". Daddy never missed a beat. He looked at that man and said, "That's funny because I was talking to the Lord last night and he didn't mention anything to me about it!"

That man's eyes got big and he simply stomped back to his car and drove away. I asked Daddy if he thought the man was mad. Daddy said, "I don't think so. He seemed like a level-headed fellow to me". I asked, "Why do you think he was level-headed?" Daddy said, "Because he had snuff running out of both corners of his mouth at the same time". RD

The Substitute

It was very unusual for us to have a substitute teacher in the little school that I attended. If a teacher was going to be absent they had to arrange for a teacher to cover for them unless it was an emergency. Well, I guess I was about eleven or so and in the fifth grade and we had a substitute teacher one day. Looking back on it I feel sorry for substitutes. We were not nice to the lady, not mean, just not nice. She passed around a sheet of paper so we could write our names and there were some unusual names on that list. She would call out the name to see which kid the name belonged to and we just laughed and laughed as some of them were quite naughty, at least for eleven year old boys a way back then. The girls were mostly just embarrassed and hid their faces. I won't repeat some of the names we wrote as I'm sure you know what they were and I'm trying to keep it clean here!

At any rate I told the teacher, whose name my part timers will not let me remember, that I was out of paper and would it be okay if I walked down to the local Mom and Pop store and get some more. The store was only about a quarter of a mile away, a five minute walk at a slow pace. She said that would be fine and I asked if Bruce could go with me. She was also agreeable to that and we left. Five minutes there, a few minutes at the store and five minutes back. Fifteen minutes max. Except there was one small problem. Neither Bruce nor I had any money. Bruce was one of the few people I knew growing up that was poorer than I was. Every time I think of Bruce I always remember my Grannie's admonition to always wear clean underwear as you never know when you'll be in a wreck! Now you may ask why I think of that particular advice. Well I'm not sure if Bruce even had any underwear and I always wondered if he was in an accident what would the ER people do. Just not treat him or what?! Just park him out back until he died and let the undertaker deal with it I guess. Very good kid and a great friend just poor. He and his family helped my grandparents out when the tornado tore the roof off their house but that's another story. What to do?

Well, we walk to the store and lo (lo, a not oft used word) we looked across the street and there was Mr. Guy Reynold's house and there was firewood scattered about in a sorta pile. The little light above my head comes on, dimly but on nonetheless and we go knock on the door.

We asked if he would like for us to finish splitting his firewood and stack it on the porch for him, for a small fee of course! Mr. Reynolds was agreeable to the tune of a quarter apiece to get the job done. We took turns splitting the wood and thankfully it was the fall of the year so not too hot. Also neither of us lost any appendages or had to go to the ER. Good thing what with Bruce and his apparent underwear problem. About an hour later we have it all split and stacked and he pays us. To the store we go.

We get sodas and a candy bar and a snack cake and still have a dime or so apiece. Bruce thought he had died and gone to heaven and insisted on spending his last dime because if he went home with it and his older brother found out about it he would beat him up and take it away from him. So another round of sodas and candy. We sat on old wooden soda cases under the covered drive in front of the store where the old men would occasionally gather and tell lies. We were alone however on that particular day. We ate and drank and thoroughly enjoyed the fruits of our labor. A very nice day as I have mentioned so we took our time. Then back to school.

Bruce and I come back into the classroom some two hours after we had left and the substitute teacher had only one thing to say to us, "Where's the paper?"! PGG

Rock Slinging and Family Pride

My father told this story to me about fifty years ago. It is a glimpse into the past and offers a bit of insight on how things have changed. My grandfather, Papa Jim, was a farmer. The crops he grew not only sustained his family but were sold to local grocery stores in and around Coosa and Tallapoosa counties. This income was used to buy necessities such as tobacco, snuff and such!

On this one particular day, somewhere around 1930, Papa Jim loaded his old wooden wagon with some produce along with my Daddy, his baby sister Katie Lee and (I think) his brother James. They made the trip to Alexander City and sold corn, peas, greens and various other farm raised items to several of the stores in that area.

Later that afternoon they were making the long mule powered wagon trip back home and stopped by an old country store. There were three or four men sitting on wooden crates outside the store whittling, chawin' tobacco and talking. One of those men was the store owner, a Mr. "Smith". (I changed his name to protect the ignorant.)

Papa Jim said, "Mr. Smith, I have a couple of watermelons left. Would you be interested in them at a fair price?" Mr. Smith, whether out of pure meanness, drankin' or just trying to show off in front of his friends said, "Get on out of here peddler and take those watermelons and those ugly kids with you!".

Papa Jim calmly replied, "Mr. Smith, if you don't want the watermelons that's just fine, but you don't need to belittle my children." That's when old man Smith said, "Well, if you will step off that wagon, I will show you a thing or two about belittling!"

Well, my grandfather stepped down from that old wagon and approached Mr. Smith. While he was doing this old man Smith stood up and grabbed a 2x4 board about three feet long. My Daddy said that it had a nail driven through it on one end.

Now before I finish this story, I have to relay my experiences with Papa Jim's prowess in rock slinging. I have seen him line a half-dozen tin cans on a cross-tie and take rocks and from thirty feet away knock each one of them off without missing. He threw side-armed and his aim was true every time.

Now, old man Smith had made about three steps toward my grandfather wielding that nail infested 2x4 board. Papa Jim calmly reached down, picked up a rock and side-armed it right into old man Smith's forehead, right between the eyes as they say in the old western movies! Knocked the old geezer out cold. The Biblical David could not have been prouder!

Papa Jim slowly got back on his wagon, looked at his kids and said, "Guess we'll be eatin' watermelon tonight" and they headed on home. RD.

TV Problems

I guess I got some of my orneriness from Papa Jim as the following story may attest to. Somewhere around late 1969 or early 1970, I was married and living in an upstairs apartment in Hoxel, Germany. Television was pretty much a luxury in those days and besides Armed Forces Network was the only programming that I could understand anyway. In an effort to 'Keep up with the Jonses', I bought a used black and white TV from one of my buddies for $10.00. He warned me that after about fifteen minutes you would have to adjust the vertical hold on it as the picture would start rolling. I put up with that for about three weeks until the adjustment on the front panel seemed to do no good. It was then that I discovered there was another set of adjustments on the rear of the TV. It got to the point that even adjusting the vertical hold on the rear of the TV did no good.

Being a real self-proclaimed genius I decided that I needed more adjustment. I took the cover off of the rear of the TV and replaced the vertical hold adjustment knob with one from an old stereo volume adjustment. Not only did I replace it, but I ran wires from the back of the TV to the volume adjustment knob so that I could adjust it from my bed. (We had the TV in our bedroom). It was probably one of the first remote control televisions in Germany at the time. The modification was flawless for about a week. Then I ran out of adjustment on my new-newfangled remote control. It began rolling again and nothing I could do would stop it.

Now back in those days, I was prone to imbibe on a pretty regular basis, had a very short fuse as far as my temper was concerned and felt that anything that didn't work needed instant 'cowboy justice'. So there I was lying in bed trying to watch TV when the picture started rolling again.

My remote control had run out of adjustment and I felt a need to do something to rectify the problem. My solution was to reach into the night-stand, pull out my pistol and render the aforesaid justice. I killed the offending TV. Yup, I shot it, I really shot it. It only made a small mess in the apartment wall. I have since matured slightly but I still get an unnatural 'twitch' in my eye even today when the TV doesn't work right!

I'm not that bad now. I have actually only shot maybe three TVs over the last forty or so years. I will say that in fifty years or so from now if anyone is exploring the woods near my house with a metal detector they may discover many items that just didn't work like I thought they should. I hate it when stuff doesn't work right. I feel it's my God given right to put it out of my misery.

I kinda have the same philosophy about people. If you work right and do what you are supposed to do then there is no problem. If not well I have this eye 'twitch' problem that bothers me from time to time. That 'twitch' problem doesn't happen often these days but when it does everyone around me seems to run away fast. I have no idea why. My wife tells me that I am just a normal guy. However she often runs and hides in the woods for three or four days at a time for no apparent reason. People are just crazy these days I guess. RD

Ms. Patti

I have known a lot of people that were in charge of things or running things. Ms. Patti was the first lady I knew to be so in charge and I mean totally in charge. She was efficient, her work was done correctly and she was in control. Ms. Patti Fleming, CFO, treasurer, bookkeeper and information center for the City of Goodwater. I worked with the City when Mr. Dan Crew was mayor and Mr. Hugh McClung was in charge of everything else from gas, water and even the potholes in the streets.

I guess my work was done well enough that the Mayor and Mr. Hugh told me that anytime I was out of school just come on down and I could work. The catch was I had to buy Mr. Hugh McClung a small Coke every morning before work started at seven am. I was tickled to be able to spend time with him every morning. He was a good man, a good friend, loved the town and wanted things done right. I really think he didn't want to answer to Ms. Patti if things went wrong. I was always puzzled how Ms. Patti could pay me out of three different accounts as some weeks we worked for the Water Board, Cemetery and Street Department! As I looked back she was always right.

Now don't get the wrong impression of Ms. Patti. She was a lady first and a really sweet lady as long as you did things correctly. Plus, she always had the pretty gold angel in her Christmas decorations on her front door. Ms. Patti was in charge of the voters list for the city as well and she guarded and protected that with all of her might. That is the reason I have to tell of this incidence.

My good friend,. Bill Dark, Amanda Dark Wilbanks' father, had married Janice Bruce and they had moved to Goodwater where I believe Janice was working for Audie Holmes in his drugstore. Audie was the mayor at that time and was running for reelection and of course Bill Dark was going to vote for him. When Bill went in to vote he was informed that his name was not on the voters list and was told he couldn't vote. Bill hadn't realized that being a registered voter in Coosa County didn't make you automatically eligible to vote in City elections without first registering there. I can just see Bill as he entered Town Hall and informed Ms. Patti that he needed to fix things so that he could vote. He wanted his name on the voters list. Ms. Patti informed him that was something that had to be done at least seven days prior to the election and he couldn't vote today.

So with his annoying smile he informed Ms. Patti that he HAD to vote today as his candidate had already paid him to! Well Ms. Patti came out from behind her desk with fire in her eyes! Bill Dark exited Town Hall rather quickly. He still laughs at the explosive look little Ms. Patti had given him and he didn't get to vote that day! CL

Crab Apple Tree

It lives on! In 1918, my grandmother, Annie Clark (Brown) Dark, planted a mail order crab apple tree at the old home place in Keno, Alabama. This was three years before my father was born (1921). I heard my dad mention that crab apple tree many times when I was a young man. He always talked about when he was growing up the crab apples were so sour that you could hardly eat them but in the spring when it bloomed the tree was so beautiful. I think my grandmother made jellies and preserves from the apples.

The old farm has changed ownership many times over the years. I had never visited the property so in 1992 I decided to find out who owned the property. At that time, Bruce Graham owned the old farm. I asked Bruce if I could visit the old home place and he graciously gave me permission. The old house was almost all gone. Just a portion of the original remained and Bruce was storing hay in that section. I wandered around the place and just away from one corner of the house, I saw what appeared to be a crab apple tree. It was weather beaten with many broken limbs. It looked as though it was almost dead. I found one little sprout that was growing from the root system. It was only about the diameter of a pencil and was perhaps eighteen inches tall. I managed to take a knife to cut through the root then dig up that sprout. I brought it home and planted it in my back yard. I had no idea that it would live.

Today, that sprout is about thirty feet tall and probably sixteen to eighteen inches in diameter at the base. It produces many large crab apples every year. Daddy was right. Those big apples are some kind of sour! However in the spring of the year for a few days, it is a beautiful sight with its pink buds that slowly turn to white blooms. Papa Jim, Mamaw and my Dad have all gone to a better place but that crab apple tree is still with us.

Here is a shot I took of it today. It leans pretty bad but seems as strong as can be. It's almost in full bloom. The photo is not the best but maybe you can get the idea. A small part of my childhood that still lives. RD

Lost Nickle

I hated to tell my sister about her bad luck but I did share. As small kids we were given a nickel a day for spending money and we spent it everyday. We loved to go to the Brown's Grocery Store that had the largest selection of candy in Goodwater. They actually had some four for a penny, a lot of three for a penny, even more two for a penny and a lot of penny candy. Martha and I would spend as much as thirty minutes making our selections. We tried to get the most pieces of candy we could for a nickel. I loved those peanut butter logs that were brittle and sweet and they were only two for a penny. One day as I was preparing to go candy shopping I ask Martha Jean if she was ready and she indicated she was not feeling well. She wanted me to buy her a nickel's worth of candy and I agreed that I would if she would give me her nickel. I put her nickel in my hand with mine and off I went. I would have secured the money in my pocket but the elastic waist shorts I wore that day had no pockets. Skipping and running down the sidewalk I was distracted by something or someone and I dropped a nickel on the sidewalk. As it rolled down the walk I was in hot pursuit.

Oh no! The nickel rolled off of the walk to the curb and into a storm drain that swallowed the nickel. I almost cried! Anyway, I went to Brown's and bought a nickels worth of four for a penny candy and hustled back home to break the bad news to Martha Jean. Arriving home Martha asked about the trip to the candy store and and I had to tell her I had lost her nickel. In lieu of getting beat up by my sister I shared my candy half and half. I never ever ask her to take my nickel and buy my candy! CL

And of course inquiring minds want to know how Charles knew that it was his sister's nickle that was lost?!

A Dark and Howling Night

It was so dark you couldn't see your hand in front of your face! I had always heard that but never believed it until that night. My boyhood friend Randy and I were walking to my house for some reason my part timers will not let me recall. Perhaps we had been at the school for a basketball game or at his house and decided to go to mine for some unknown pursuit. Why we were on the road doesn't really matter I guess. We were there and it was dark. The use of the word road is not exactly accurate. It was dirt. About a car and a half wide and had not been scraped recently.

I guess I need to elaborate about road scraping. The county had road scrapers that they would send around sporadically to kinda even out all the ruts and gulleys. Most folks call them graders nowadays but we called them scrapers back then as that is what they did. It was a big event when they would come by as not much happened back in the woods where we lived. The grader would come over the hill amid much excitement amongst my sister from Hell and myself. He would eventually return for the grading of the other side of the road. As I mentioned it was about a car and a half wide so it required two trips of the scraper to get it all evened out.

I devised a plan once where I constructed a sled of left over lumber from somewhere and an old rope. The idea was that when the scraper came by I would hook up to the back of it as there was a hitch thingie there and ride to my hearts content. It was a great plan. Except that there no way to communicate with the guy who ran the scraper plus he didn't even know I was there to start with! Also I was slowly getting father and father away from home with no way to get back except walking. This kinda detracted from the riding thing. A great plan but not well thought out looking back on it. I have often wondered what the man thought when he discovered what was left of my contraption! Sorry, got a little distracted there!

When I say dark I mean dark like you have never seen which is kinda oxymoronic when you think about it as you can't really see dark. It was about nine at night and a new moon. Also it was cloudy so there were no stars. We were just to the left of the middle of nowhere so there were no street lights or any other ambient light of any kind! No light at all. We are walking along with no flashlights or any other source of illumination.

We are crossing over the top of this hill so you can kinda but not really make out where the sides of the road are. We are mostly going by feel. If the road starts to dip either left or right you are in the ditch so alter course!

Now it is bad enough that we can't see but there are various animals and such in the surrounding woods not to mention the Woofit! We are also approaching a creek that the Woofit is known to frequent but that's another story. We do not mention any of this as it is an unwritten law that these things are not spoken of at times like these! They are fine during the day or around a nice campfire at night with others but not now, not here! We start down this big hill near the creek and the canopy of trees engulfs us. It is even darker than before if possible. I put my hand in front of my face and I cannot see it at all. I move it back and forth, front to back and nothing! No shadows, no hint of movement, no nothing! It really is that dark!

Did I also mention that there might be snakes in the road that we can't see? Or 'possums, or foxes or Woofits?! Randy and I are quietly exchanging small talk and whistling by the graveyard so to speak when all of a sudden there is this God awful howl! A really loud howl for no reason at all except to scare the sh. . .uh. . .stuff out of two young boys in the dark. We can't run as we can't see where we are going! Basically we freeze until we finally figure out that it is one of the dogs at the house that is nearby where we are passing. One of their dogs took exception to our small talk and whistling I suppose. At least we convinced ourselves that it was a dog.

Fortunately the creek was just ahead for the impromptu washing of various undergarments! No Woofit in sight not that we could have seen him anyway! PGG

Charles relates the following about a Banshee.

The Night of the Banshee!

When my son, Chase, was about eight or so he had a sleep over birthday party and he had about six or eight rascals that came over and celebrated with him. After they had torn the basketball goal set down and had a cookout with hamburgers and such they wanted to hear a scary story from me.

As we gathered in a circle in the backyard I told them I had an incident that I would tell them but no stories. All of this was true I said. However, it wasn't but they didn't know that. I told them that my family had lived on this farm for many, many years and there had been some mysterious happenings and deaths on this farm including my baby sister.

It all happened one day in the late, late summer or actually early fall as cotton picking time was upon us and we all had to pick cotton. My mama taught school and my daddy had other jobs but it was time to pick the cotton. Mama would put baby Sara Leigh on a pallet at the end of each cotton row and would tend to her when she returned down from the next row. Mama had heard Sara Leigh whine a little but thought nothing of it but she went to check on her anyway. When she got there little Sara Leigh was still and lifeless and of course we were all nervous, sad and excited about little Sara Leigh. Their was not one mark on her body that we could see. Sara Leigh was quickly carried to the emergency room at the hospital in Alex City.

The doctors determined that all of the blood in her little body was gone and there were two small holes in the base of her neck where the blood had exited her body. It was all kept really quiet in the public. My parents knew what had happened as it had happened to almost every generation of our family. I told them I could carry them up to the cemetery and show them where three of ours had died for unknown causes in one year. They had all died in the late summer and all by the mouth and fangs of the Banshee.

I knew I had them as all of their eyes were as big as saucers and they were all taking deep breaths. I told them that they should not worry because it was known that the Banshee would not go inside of a house or enter a stream of water to take a victim. Furthermore, I had never seen the Banshee other than possibly some of its tracks. However it was always said that if you ever did see it you would know it and would never forget it if you made it to safety. As I looked around the circle I noticed that it had gotten smaller and the boys were sitting closer together and looking at each other for safety. Even Chase was on the hook. As I got up from sitting on the ground I stretched my arms behind my back and screamed at the top of my voice, " OH LORD THERE IT IS!"

I broke for the back door and all of them jumped up and they were tight behind me. The next to the last boy slung the door shut and locked it leaving little Will Neighbors locked out of the house and he was scratching on the door pretty loud to get in! Well, when I unlocked and opened the door all I could see was the whites of his eyes and he grabs the door and pushes with all of his might. The bad thing is the door knob didn't quit going until it hit the wall inside the kitchen by the refrigerator. As the old saying goes "That boy needed some relief!" and he got it.

They all slept in a corner in the den and in one sleeping bag I believe! I could have gone in there about five in the morning and screamed and we would not have had a single window left. They stayed up until about four as it was. During the night I heard one of them bet another one in the group, "I bet you five dollars you wont go outside and use the bathroom!" There were no takers! I guess they were afraid of the Banshee! CL

Class Trip to Washington D.C.

The classes of 1960 and 1961 made the first class trip to Washington, D.C. during our Spring Break in March of 1960. I believe the week's trip cost $100, which included our bus transportation, lodging for six or seven nights and all of our meals! Brookie and Pat Heard were recruited to be our chaperones.

We spent the first night somewhere along the way and caused so much of a ruckus that the hotel called our next stop to warn them about us. We didn't do anything destructive. We were just running in and out of each others rooms and stuff like that. We probably had four to a room and were so excited that sleep was not a priority. This was probably the first time that some in the group had ever been out of the state of Alabama.

We saw all the sights in D.C. including a tour of the White House, a visit to Arlington, the Capitol, Mount Vernon, Monticello and several other places. I remember that the local tour guide insulted us by saying he was taking us to a fabulous place to shop and it was a glorified five and dime store. It had an escalator and he thought that would be our first experience with one.

On our way home, we went through the Great Smoky Mountains in North Carolina. The weather turned icy and it was dangerous to drive the bus on the roads. We had to balance the weight on both sides of the bus and it was pretty scary for a while as we descended.

There were lots of other school groups making this trip and a group from Florence, Alabama was in our hotel in D.C. Linda Richardson met a guy from Florence and they were 'a couple' for a while, going to each others prom, etc. A couple of college guys from D.C. tried to get a couple of us to leave our hotel and go out with them. It was very tempting but we couldn't get permission from Brookie and Pat to leave with them. Looking back, I realize that this could have been a horrible thing but back then we didn't worry that much about strangers.

I had a big group picture of us in front of the White House but I can't find it. I believe we ran into some snow/slush on our trip which was shown in that photo. I believe the classes of 1962 and 1963 took this trip in the spring of 1962 and they may have been the last classes that got to do this. BDB

Jerry McEwen adds this to the story. The CCHS Class of 1960 had our senior trip to Washington the same week as the Goodwater Classes of 1960 and 1961. We have the large pictures of each. They are fun to look at. We stayed in different hotels and had separate tour schedules except for a night together at the Lotus Club. The two groups sat on opposite sides of the room. My wife Sandra and I remember it well because after a breakup in January, we kind of made up (at least a little bit) that night when I went across the room and asked Sandra Thomas to dance with me. Lucky for me, we have now been married over fifty-two years. Gotta love class trips!

Speeding Ticket

Mr. Vance Wheeler back in the day was the guy you went to
if you got a speeding ticket. One Sunday night back in about 1963, I
had just left the evening services at the Kellyton Methodist Church
and I was driving my Dad's 1954 Chevrolet. I was able to finally
drive legally but I always took the round-about way home and of
course had to test the speed of the car. I was heading home on
U.S.280 somewhere around the Dallas Forbus home and for some
reason the State Troopers had set up the dreaded radar!

Back in those days, the radar consisted of a fairly big box
sitting on the side of the road and a trooper lying in the grass would
read the speed results. He would radio ahead to the troopers just
down the road and they would pull you over for a ticket. Well, I got
pulled over at the intersection of 115 and 280 for doing sixty-five at
night. I guess I was a regular speed demon. A way back in those
days we had speed limits for day and night driving. I want to say that
the day time speed limit was sixty and the night time limit was fifty
or maybe fifty-five. The speed limit signs actually changed when
headlights hit them at night.

I didn't want my Daddy to know that I had gotten a speeding
ticket because he would ground me for quite a while, perhaps for
life. I was a mental wreck worrying about that speeding ticket and
waited until the last day possible to go visit the dreaded Justice of
the Peace, Mr. Vance Wheeler. I walked into Mr. Wheeler's office
which was next to the theater with my head down and my ticket in
my hand. He said, "Son, are you Bobby Dark's boy?" I admitted that
I was. He gave me a long speech on how speeding could get me
killed and that breaking the law was a bad thing. I nodded and
simply said, "Yes Sir, I know".

Then he asked me if we did upholstery work at my Dad's
shop. I told him that we occasionally put on seat covers for folks. At
that time, Mr. Wheeler had a 1954 Ford Sedan. He asked if I could
help him get a deal on putting on some seat covers for his old Ford. I
told him that I certainly would be glad to put seat covers on his car
and that I would talk to Daddy about giving him a good deal. I was
desperate because I had waited until the last day to pay my ticket and
I only had twenty dollars in my pocket. That was my life's savings at
the time which is pretty much my life's savings now!

He said, "Son, I am going to help you out here. You give me $15.00 for the ticket and I will be talking to you and your Dad soon about my seat covers". I gladly paid the money, but poor old Mr. Wheeler never made it to my Dad's shop for the seat covers and old Butchie Boy escaped the wrath of being grounded again. I lived to speed again! RD

Pimento Cheese and Celery Sticks

Why I got banned from the dinner table! I was just reading an interesting article about pimento cheese and the different ways to prepare it and eat it in sandwiches or as a dip. One of my Dad's favorite ways to eat it was on celery sticks. I have to admit I am partial to it also. Now, when I was about fifteen or sixteen years old I had reached a point in my worldly knowledge that far exceeded any of my teachers or my parents. It's just amazing how smart a young man becomes in such a short time and I thought I was on top of my game.

However, at school, I had been forced into a class called Literature. It was all about plays, poems and other such jibberish that was written quite a few years before I ever came on to the scene. I couldn't understand what those dudes were trying to get across with all the thee, thou and several other words that I still don't get. My report card reflected that I either suffered from some type of brain malfunction or I just didn't give a darn about literature.

Charles Luker related he had a classmate from over Hanover way named Billie! He was a good ole boy but school was in his way and he also had a bit of trouble with literature. Mrs. DeGraffenried required all the students to learn a poem every six weeks. Poor ole Billie was just struggling trying to learn one line. When he got up to recite the poem he would give the title and the first line and then it was over. He would double his fist up and knock himself in the head and it sounded like a woodpecker! He appeared to have it up there somewhere and he was trying to knock it back in place. I'm sure sweet Mrs. Betty DeGraffenried Burgess passed him anyway because he tried so hard.

Anyway, one Sunday after church my Mom had made a meal fit for a king. All the fixin's were there including pimento cheese on celery sticks. Prior to sitting down for Sunday dinner (that's what we called the noon meal, supper was the evening meal, we didn't have lunch) my Dad had been reviewing my recent report card and was really giving me a hard time about my literature grade. He espoused on and on about how important it was to be well-rounded in all aspects of my education. At that time, since I was way smarter than he was, I just got more and more set in my mind that I didn't need any danged literature! I was determined to rebel and show him.

We sat down for our wonderful Sunday dinner and my Dad began eating. Every time he would bite one of those celery sticks it sounded like somebody was chewing on dry corn or maybe eating broken glass. In my rebellious way, I threw up a hand and said quite loudly, "Hark, dost thou hearest yon horse?" Well, my Dad didn't find that statement very amusing and stopped chewing long enough to say, "You are finished with dinner and you are excused from the table". (That meant that my meal was over and I had better get up and away from the table NOW!). I think I had to eat alone for about a week as I had been banned. I learned that I was not quite ready to take on my Dad in the 'Attitude' department. Seems he had the upper hand! RD

The Barn

One of the places I loved when I was growing up was the old barn that was about a hundred yards in front of my grandparent's house. When I was young we had a cow that was kept there at night and where we (read Grannie) milked her. Two stalls were on the left side and a large area about the size of a garage next to that and a room in the back for feed, supplies, junk and such. The ceiling of that room was the floor in the loft where I spent most of my time. It had been used to store hay at one time but no more. As the old folks got older the barn was no longer used except by me for my many adventures.

The back side of the barn did not have any openings so I made one with an old hatchet I found. It was a porthole so to speak so that I could look out on the world behind the barn and protect it from all enemies foreign and domestic. When I say foreign I mean aliens and not the illegal kind! It was also good for observing if any scurvy dogs were trying to attack my stern like my sister from Hell!

Because the barn was on a small hill and the loft was about twelve feet up above that there was almost always a breeze flowing through the area and it was somewhat cooler up there. I have spent many an hour there with books I had gotten from the bookmobile but that's another story. I would sit on the floor with my back against the wall and time and space could no longer hold me in its grip. I was free and lived many an adventure through the pages that transported me to worlds both known and unknown. I don't believe a video game can do that for you.

I would allow visitors to my sanctuary on occasion but they never seemed to share in the wonder of it like I did. To them it was just an old barn. Try as I might I could not convince them of its wonders. We did have some good times there and even a few sex education classes using the time honored educational method of 'show and tell' with a few young girls who shall for obvious reasons remain nameless.

I once built a high tech radar/communications console for my barn fortress. It consisted of some old boards, some purloined junk auto dashboard parts and a lot of imagination. It could receive signals from Mars and beyond. Flash Gordon had nothing on me! I patrolled oceans and deep space and lost cities and discovered more treasures and relics than I could ever spend or enjoy. While the old barn wasn't a hopped up DeLorean it could still transport me through time both forward and backwards. I would sometimes dress the part with my wooden shields and swords or laser zappers. Pirate hat or space helmet was optional!

Back when the barn had the cow and hay and feed and such we had rats and mice that frequented the area. I would take my old BB gun up there and sit quietly and have a 'rat killin'! The Great White Hunter stealthily hiding in a corner waiting on the alien-rat hybrids to emerge from their pods! I might get one or two but it was a futile effort. Even the occasional chicken snake couldn't keep up with them. When we no longer had the cow or the feed all the animals went away in search of greener pastures so to speak. Even after the hay and feed had long ago left the smell lingered as long as the barn did. It had that sweet smell of decaying grass that I guess all old barns have. I can close my eyes and almost breathe in that wonderful aroma even today!

I remember coming back to the old place many years later and the barn was no longer there. I figured it had fell in and I walked up there and looked around. There were no boards or tin or any evidence that the barn had ever been there except for the bare patch of earth where it had once stood. Don't now what happened to it and never asked. The most logical explanation was that without my vigilance the aliens had zapped it into space to use for their own nefarious reasons. Perhaps they were trying to reverse engineer my advanced radar/comm system! PGG

Coach, Chemistry and Fireworks

It was the school year 1965-66 and the Junior-Senior Classes made up the chemistry class under Coach Hayes. One day coach was going to show us how phosphorus would burn at room temperature. The phosphorus was stored in a solution in a jar and I believe it was some type of oil as phosphorus will spontaneously react with the oxygen in the air. He reaches in the jar with a set of tongs and pulls out a piece of the phosphorus and it did not readily react and ignite. So he sticks a lighted match to the phosphorus and it not only ignited but exploded and a piece spewed off! Yep! Right on Pat Hawkins Cofield's sweater and starts burning a hole in it! Pat grabs the stuff and it burns her hand and coach is jumping around like a Japanese shortstop trying to grab the stuff. He finally got it in hand and it didn't burn his old tough, calloused hands. He was frightened as we all were that Pat was hurt. After all pain and injury was established and soothed we all had a big laugh! Everyone but coach! We encouraged Pat to wear her ruined sweater every time we had a chemistry test to be assured of an 'A'. Of course, she didn't need that as she was smart anyway.

Ole coach was a pistol ball. He would sit behind his desk with his feet resting on top of his desk showing off his everyday unmatched socks. He had purchased a truck load of nylon socks from Camp Seibert. We used them for football practice and he had saved a few hundred pair for his use. The socks came in the colors of OD green and beige and coach would wear one color of each everyday. I believe it was Ed Sprayberry that asked him one day where he got his socks. Without hesitation, coach responded, "I don't knoooowwww but I got another pair at home just like them!" We had a lot of fun and a lot of funny experiences in chemistry. One day coach was getting after all of us about not trying to even learn this stuff and I believe it was Scotty Rogers who told him that Judy Forbus had used his book the two years before and she had learned everything out of it! Coach's response was I'm gonna tear y'alls grades up! CL

Betty says she took chemistry as a junior and chemistry was not Coach Hayes' best subject. We all loved him to death, but he struggled nearly as much as we did trying to figure out what was going on. One day he could not get the answers to some problems to come out right and match up with the answers that were given in the answer book.

His response was to throw the answer book away and say that it was flawed. Mike Swindall and I were both in the class and Mama told me in later years that Coach Hayes would come in the teachers' lounge before school many days and ask, "Did Betty or Mike work out the problems for homework last night? They were pretty tough." Some of the more scientifically smart students in the class (not me!) usually wound up explaining how to solve them. That was group learning at its finest! Thankfully Mama didn't make me take physics the next year! Maybe by the time you took it, Charlie, he had been through the course enough times to master it. BDB

The summer before my junior year coach did go to school and take some chemistry and physic courses and did a pretty good job. As a senior we had a practice teacher from Auburn and he was really good. An Atkinson fellow from Sylacauga. Our class was really lucky as I learned a lot and appreciated Mr. Atkinson's efforts. Coach was pretty easy to get off subject and start talking about his minnow ponds and he and Gene Hayes and COW crappie fishing. He used to privately hound me about a good place to squirrel hunt. CL

Four and Sixty

When I was just a puppy I looked so forward to going to the lake or swimming at Russell Pool (that was before Goodwater's pool). The thing I really looked forward to was stopping at the Dairy Queen on Washington Street (the four lane) in Alex City. We all got a small cone of ice cream and it was delicious. As soon as we purchased a cone we got in the car and headed toward Goodwater with all four windows on the car rolled down. You had to do some fast licking on those cones of ice cream with the cute little curl on the top as the summer heat was hot and the wind blowing on you just made it melt faster. If you slowed down for just a second you would find that delicious cream running down on your hand and your arm too. I would just lick it off as I didn't have a shirt on anyway and I guess my sisters did. I wouldn't have noticed then anyway.

It took about two miles of travel to consume the delight, cone and all. I do remember a small cone was a nickel and a large cone was a dime. For another nickel they would dip it in a vat of chocolate and you would have a dipped cone. The chocolate was warm and it made the ice cream melt faster as I got to try that one time and it just wasn't worth it. If you drop some on the floor mat in the car you just washed it out with a hose as all the floors were vinyl-rubber and easily cleaned.

I remember one Sunday afternoon Mother, my sister Martha Jean, Martha's good friend Nikki McGraw and Old Charlie Boy was headed to Alex City for something or maybe just riding around. Nikki McGraw was sort of a city girl and had never been around cows or any farm animals. We were going by my Uncle Charlie Corley's house and his cows were grazing near the highway. All of a sudden Nikki said look! That cow has his tail sticking straight out! I starting laughing because I knew what was fixing to take place and it did and Nikki looked so surprised at the event.

How did I get this mixed up with eating ice cream? We all just had simple fun back then and enjoyed the breeze from the rolled down windows that we referred to as four and sixty air conditioning. Remember those little 'wind wing' windows that you could turn to blow directly on you if you were in the front seat? Four windows down and sixty miles an hour! CL

The Sockhop

One of the big things we had when I was growing up was a sockhop. For those uneducated or from up North, but I repeat myself, this is a dance held in the school gym and as street shoes were banned on the gym floor everybody had to remove their shoes. Thus sockhop! The reason shoes were banned were they would bring dirt on the floor and the soles were harder than the varnish finish and would wear it down thus resulting in a refinish job and big bucks. The only thing allowed on the floor was tennis shoes and socks. Tennis shoes are called sneakers nowadays and I guess those air shoes that are big bucks to buy. Never knew why they were called tennis shoes as no one I knew played tennis even though tennis courts were built at my school shortly before I graduated. Remember my shoes were somewhere south of ten dollars which was big money back then. The shoes at the time were mostly black and white high tops although you could get red ones that were low cut. Still have an old pair around here somewhere that I bought at a thrift store a few years ago.

Well anyway we had a sockhop a few times a year. The biggie was after the football homecoming game. Occasionally there would be one to help support a local charity event or something. Cost was usually about a quarter to attend and the music was supplied by a portable record player most times. I have been to a few where we were encouraged to bring our own records as the sponsoring group didn't have a varied selection. Pay to get in and listen to your own records! But there were girls there!

We actually had what one would call a garage band now play at a few of our hops. It was local kids from school and they would play and during the break out would come the aforementioned record player. Don't know if they got payed or not or just did it for the experience and the hope of fame and fortune! I remember dancing with a certain someone to the songs and would love to go back and have five minutes of that over again! We usually knew most everybody at The Hop as most called it. There was even a song by that title by Danny and the Juniors a way back in 1958! Occasionally someone would show up that we did not know. Usually caused some consternation amongst the locals. Who is that, why are they here, etc. Usually just a friend of a friend or a visiting cousin or some such. Much drama for such a small community but there wasn't much else to talk about.

Well there was that girl that had to quit school and go live with her aunt for some unexplained reason. And Billy was no longer around and some thought he had gone off to the war but he was only fifteen! And Julie's mom and Timmy's dad and, well, you get the idea. Just a little Peyton Place.

We would occasionally have a 'formal' dance there. The girls would come up with a theme and decorate with crepe paper and such. A 'real' band might even be hired to play for the event. Everybody would dress up and the girls had corsages and the whole nine yards as it were. We didn't have limos and such that seem to be the rage nowadays but we had fun and thought we were 'uptown'!

Dance at the old gym. Photo courtesy Ray Hornsby

Gonna go walking around town with Charles and a few others.

Goodwater East Side

Starting on the south end of Goodwater there was the Methodist Church. Next you had three homes that included City Clerk Patti Fleming and the Harris Home. Next there was an old service station that I believe was owned by the Hawkins. Next door there was the Old Hickory Cafe with the running pig sign and it had several operators over the years and while I don't remember his name he was allegedly a member of the KKK!

Continuing there was Mr. J. Walter Robinson's Pure or Union 76 Service Station that was a full service establishment. You could get tires, oil change, lube, car wash, gas with oil checked, windshield washed and tires checked. His able cashier Ms. Mary Vaughn was always a joy to see!

Just behind the Old Hickory was Mr. Clark Stewart's garage where Mr. Stewart and his son had a thriving business. After Mr. Clark Stewart's death, Tom Stewart took over. They were both good mechanics regardless of what Mr. Tom always said. He stated he wasn't a real mechanic, he was just a good parts replacer. His wife, Mrs. Margaret June, was the bookkeeper and she was absolutely precious. I believe the building was owned by the Gilliland Family.

Next there was a small strip mall that had had two or three stores in it. I remember the building but never remember it being open. It was in front of the Gilliland House and another duplex house. I believe Mrs. Suggs, the first grade teacher, lived in the left side part and Mr. and Mrs. Steve Gilliland, Jr. lived in the right side.

Moving along there was a house and a chiropractors office where Billy Phillips and Judy Phillips lived. Judy was the daughter of Mr. and Mrs. Penton Humphrey and the sister of Huey Humphrey. They were great friends of mine and I was treated as if I had been their child. They had a small concrete goldfish pond in the front yard and I fished in it all of the time as they watched from their front porch. They laughed so hard at my antics while trying to get a bite from one of the fish. I actually caught one of the goldfish after much effort.

A very large house was next and it was the home and dental office of Dr. McClendon. I did not know him very well. He scared me! He was sort of tall and his veins were very visible in his hands. I'm sure he was a good man and all but he still scared me. There were other dentists in the area over time. One of my two front teeth on top was loose and daddy carried me up to Dr. Crew's house. He put me in a dentist chair and pulled it and before I knew it he had grabbed the other one and yanked it out. It hurt! He said it needed pulling anyway. He charged twenty-five cents. I was so mad I could have hit him! Betty DeGraffenried Burgess says the school dentist once pulled several of her teeth and put them in something and said to take them home to her mama. She was less than thrilled because she was not sure all of them were loose, so she went to another dentist in Alex City.

Next up you had a street or alley that went to The Southern Casket Company. It was owned by the Gilliland family and was run by Joe Gilliland and Steve Jr. They employed several people and it was always a source for us kids to get an old casket top to use as a snow sled for the few snow accumulations that we had. I think Mr. E. Phelps Bridges was a mainstay in the business and may have been part owner. At one time there was a park or playground behind the casket factory and one of my most exciting memories was of a Vacation Bible School picnic there once. It had a stream and really big pecan trees as best I recall. As a small lad and a member of the Goodwater Presbyterian Church I was involved in a lot of church activities. I guess my mama saw the need.

I remember the preacher was name Augenbaugh or something like that. I called him Mr. Organ Bald and he answered to that too. I believe he was bald! The VBS had lasted two weeks I assume and on the last day there was a picnic scheduled. It was to be held at the Goodwater Casket Company Park. I remember leaving our church and marching single file past the Methodist Church, the Baptist Church and then through town to enter the park. It was a really neat place that had sky high pecans trees, a small stream that ran through the park and wooden picnic tables. What happened after that I have no idea as I just have a memory flashback of friends marching single file by the churches and then going in the park. That had to be in 1953 or 1954. Childhood flashback I guess!

Just over from the casket factory was The Alabama Power Company Office. I know they sold appliances and that is where most folks went to pay their power bill. Ms. Ressie Smith was the clerk and I remember I once gave her our check for the amount of about seven dollars or so for our monthly light bill! Then there was the original Chapman 5 & 10 and I was always so impressed by how much stock they had available for sale.

Near there was Jeff Sprayberry's barber shop. Mr. Sprayberry had an air conditioned shop and was always busy. If you ever wanted to find Gilmer "Roonie" Thomas that was a good place to look. Roonie was a Mr. Fix-It. Betty Degraffenried Burgess says she remembers her Mama getting him to fix things at the house from time to time. She also says he and Robert Smith were good friends and he was best man when Robert and Faye Smith married. The minister met both Robert and Roonie for the first time right before the ceremony and he called out Roonie's name instead of Robert's during the ceremony.

They were all nervous and no one would correct him. Faye always said she was really married to Roonie! Roonie visited the barbershop several times a day to keep up with the goings on! Next Mrs. Lynna Sprayberry had a beauty shop and on Thursday afternoon, Friday and Saturday mornings it was the busiest place in town. Women were always leaving her shop smiling. That was the day of the big hairdo! Women getting ready for church you know!

The original Western Auto Store was beside it but after they moved across the street I do not recall the occupant. Next Mrs. J. R. Wingfield had a really nice gift shop next to the library. She was always so nice and sweet and ready to help you or let you browse. This was my favorite place to Christmas shop as they had model cars. That was also the place to carry your film for quick development, too. Mrs. Wingfield could always show you what you needed to buy to make you sweetheart happy and she wrapped it for you too! Mrs. Wingfield was always so quiet, smiling and happy and she made you feel like she had been waiting on you to come in and shop. You could call the shop a little upscale for the time but I remember that on the immediate left after you entered she had a good collection of model cars, model airplanes and model ships that most boys loved putting together. Mr Wingfield was a photographer and took many photos at his studio in the jewelry store.

Next up was the Public Library and Mrs. J.R. Gilbert was the librarian and I spent a lot of time there. I read the book "Little Black Sambo"so many times. I enjoyed the story of the tigers chasing him and finally they melted into butter and his mother made pancakes and used the butter. It went something like that anyway. I would gladly pay a handsome price for that book but I'm sure it has deteriorated to nothing plus it would not be PC today!

Mayor and Mrs. A.O. Holmes operated the Goodwater Drug Store and it was a favorite for most kids, teenagers and Bill Dark! There was a soda fountain, fountain made cokes, ice cream and snow cones! Betty says she remembers going to Goodwater Drug Store nearly every afternoon after school and getting a cherry coke and putting salted peanuts in it. What a delight! Mrs. Clintelle always enjoyed getting after us younger kids and would laugh at us most of the time. She would even let us sit on the bottom shelf of their comic book rack and read the comic books. I remember Janice Bruce working there and fixing all the sodas and she was the reason Bill Dark visited frequently. Eventually they married! Later Mr. Audie moved up the street to a new building that housed his drug store on one side and the Shop Easy Food Store on the other side. I delivered groceries for the Shop Easy Food Store operated by Mr. McDuff Stewart, Pamela Kellogg's father. I went in so many house and put groceries on the table and in the refrigerator.

No one locked their doors back then! Always enjoyed Mrs. Jarvis's delivery as she would give me fresh baked brownies! Diane Jackson Alford remembers Mrs. G.G. Jarvis making brownies with colored marshmallows that were then covered with chocolate! Oh so good.

When he moved, Mr. Frank Nail renovated the building and installed about thirty coin operated washing machines, several dryers and he could dry clean some items too. Next there was the U. S. Post Office and the Postmaster was Mr. Lewis Buttram! He had a couple of able staff members which included Alene Hawkins. That was the day of the three cent stamp and I imagine most folks got there mail from the rural mail carriers as they do today. I remember our P. O. Box # as 112 and it stayed that way for us for 60 years. I couldn't open it as I had no key but when I walked up to the window Ms. Alene would hand me our mail! The great thing about all of Goodwater was that everyone new everyone and usually by our first name! Betty also relates the following story.

Once when I was at camp, I wrote a post card to my grandaddy with whom we lived. I addressed it to "Gran, Goodwater, Alabama," and he got it!

We had a Masonic Lodge above it but I never attended! Then there was the Goodwater Police Station and the fire station. I remember the fire alarm switch was on the right and above the entrance door of the police office.

That was the only way of notifying the community that there was a fire and help was needed. I remember in the early 1950s my Uncle Cliff Rogers was a city councilman and they bought a new 1954 Dodge Fire Truck. It was in service for many years and was used to fight a lot of house fires. Maybe in the late 1960s there was a formal VFD formed and was well participated in by a lot of men. Of course the calaboose was behind the police department and was a rather study structure. It survived the many fires that Mr. Percy Glenn started!

Next door was where Mr. Holmes had moved the Drug Store and Mr. McDuff Stewart operated the Shop Easy Food Store where I worked. Mr. Mac and Mrs. Ruby operated the store for many years. Mr. Mac was the town's Fire Chief and he gained his experience in the Navy as a fireman at Pensacola Air Station. It was during WWII but he did not go to the Pacific.

Mr. Forrest Sewell's father had a grocery store next door. I remember Mr. Forrest working in the store at times and his brother Julian Sewell. I believe Julian acquired a motor scooter that had a boxed in compartment on front of the vehicle that would hold two small chairs and I remember him giving Charlie Sewell and myself a ride in that contraption. I have talked with Charlie about the rides but he doesn't remember it as he was really young and Julian doesn't remember either. Maybe someone had just loaned it to him for a short while! One of the unique things about Goodwater was that all merchants extended credit and almost all bills were paid either weekly or monthly!

Lastly former State Representative Charles Franklin owned and operated a Feed and Seed Store. He sold seed, feed, fertilizer, lime and coal and so many of the locals depended on him for the credit he offered in order to put a crop in. Mr. Franklin bought pecans from us boys and always paid us a fair price and it always depended on the market and the quality of the pecans.

At times we were shocked at what he would pay us. I always trusted him. He took over the business from his father R. N. Franklin.

Going around the corner Mr. Bobby Dark had an auto repair shop and the building had been Robert Smith Auto. Mr. Dark had a thriving business as well as all of the repair shops did. I believe you could actually drive all the way through his shop. He was assisted by his able son Butch as we all called him but he is Robert Dark Jr. I guess all of the men in the Dark family were good mechanics.

Next across the street there was a another wash house and I believed it was owned by Charles Rush. It was not as big as the other downtown wash house but it was always busy.

Goodwater West

Goodwater was once a thriving town where many families made a good living operating stores in downtown. Right now we will focus on the west side of downtown Goodwater!

On the north end of all of the contiguous buildings Mr. Dobbs had a corner barber shop and he gave me my first 'Flat Top' haircut along with my purchase of the pink 'Butch' hair wax in a small jar. Next was the Eris Theater that was first operated by Mr. Frank Nail. The theater ran shows about five nights out of the week and popcorn was five cents and a coke was five cents and the admission was fifteen cents for all under twelve years of age and then increased to thirty-five cents for over age twelve.

If you went to a rerun you were admitted for free and you usually bought popcorn and a coke for a dime. Tommy Dark remembers going to see 'The Bridge on the River Kwai' at the old theater in Goodwater. He was only ten years old in 1957 but remembers that movie as one of the best ever shown. Most of the shows we went to in that old theater were grade B movies. Dracula, The Return of Dracula and The Blob were a few that I remember.

The next store was a hardware store operated by Mr. Omer Burnette. It was always interesting to go in his store as he had white rats for sale. I always enjoyed watching the rats run through the tumbler. They ran really hard but really didn't go anywhere as the tumbler turned to match their speed. Kinda like some people I know!

Then there was the Pool Room that was operated by Mr. Arthur Colvard and later by Mr. Ted Peoples and then Mr. Walker Richardson. We enjoyed shooting pool there on Saturdays and after school and I guess it was considered a form of gambling as the loser paid ten cents for the game. I remember Mr. Vance Wheeler shooting a lot while he waited to be summoned to hold JP Court for speeding tickets issued by the Highway Patrol. They were always guilty as he did not get a fee if they were deemed innocent! His office was actually between the Eris Theater and Mr. Dobbs barbershop. I believe the pool room was owned by Louis Crew, Jr.

Next up was a grocery store owned and operated by Mr. W.M. Pruet and his sweet wife Mrs. Lee. Mr. Pruet always parched peanuts and a lot of people bought them on Saturday. His soft drink cooler was filled with cold water and a small pump cooled and circulated the water. If you took to long to get your drink you could almost freeze your hand it seemed! Drinks were a nickle and a six pack of soft drinks sold for twenty-five cents plus deposit. Then there was a bank that later became Dr. Joe Tom Roberts dentist office where I spent some miserable times.

Moving down the sidewalk was Swindall's Grocery that was owned and operated by Mr. John and Fletcher Swindall and they were famous for their hamburger meat and air conditioned store. Betty DeGraffenried Burgess remembers being able to order groceries from Swindall's and have them delivered. All of the doors were unlocked so they'd just pull the truck up in the back yard and leave the grocery sacks on the kitchen table. If anything needed to be refrigerated, they'd put it in the refrigerator for you. Simpler times.

The next store below Swindall's Grocery was Richard Neighbors' Drug Store and if my memory is right he had the first air conditioned store in Goodwater and it was always so neat and well lighted.

The next store is a store that most have forgotten! Mr. and Mrs. Rozelle had a small grocery store and they were the grandparents of Martha and Ellen Yarbrough.

The longest store operated in Goodwater was probably Crew's Clothing. The first owner was E. Louis Crew Sr., then Louis Crew Jr. and then Johnny Watson. It was a big store and you could get well attired and fitted. Shoes to under drawers.

If you needed your duds cleaned then there was a dry cleaners operated by Mr. Bud Gilliland and later Mr. Dan Crew. You could get your shirts laundered and you suits dry cleaned and the prices were reasonable.

Next was Peoples Trust and Savings bank and I remember Mr. Bill Wright as President and Jerry Anderson was a VP. Cynthia was Mr. Wright's daughter as I remember. Jerry was an exceptional tennis player and tried to teach Walt Dowdle and I how to play. This is the bank that was robbed in the 1960s.

Then there was the staple of almost every Southern town, the Western Auto Store owned and operated by James, Jessie and Mrs. Ruth Hamil. During my late teenage years I was fortunate enough to work at the Goodwater Western Auto Store. Mr. Jessie, Mrs. Ruth and children James, Jana and Janice were the owners and they always hired two or three boys during Christmas break. Our primary job was to put together bicycles, tricycles, pedal cars, kids kitchen toys, etc. They sold a lot of those toys to a lot of people in a ten mile or so radius of Goodwater. People shopped at home back then. It was not hard work other than the fact that the bicycles were stored about five doors down the street from the store and we had to bring them back to put them together. We were watched by the stern eye of Mr. Jessie and the always smiling Mrs. Ruth. We aggravated James every chance we got but he handled it well.

We always fought over who was not going to have to put the pedal cars together! They were knuckle "busters" and the boy with the least seniority usually got that job! Seniority, heck we didn't even know what that meant! It was pretty hectic as we did stay busy and James would tell us every few minutes we were getting behind. They sold a big assortment of toys, TVs, games, footballs, basketballs, basket ball goals, guns and just about everything else.

Christmas Eve was a busy day but the fun was later in the night when we started delivering Santa Claus to all the families. It was so much fun and quite rewarding to be out on Christmas Day and see a kid with his new bike that Santa Claus had given him and knowing that you had put it together. You could stop and talk to the kid and he would explain all about the bike and how fast it would go. It was just a heart warming feeling even for a teenager to know that you had done something special for a kid to help him love and remember the joy of Christmas.

The thing that touched me the most was seeing a parent make a big sacrifice to buy their kid a bicycle or a basketball. They were teaching the kids love and that Christmas was a special time for joy. We just hope that the real joy of Christmas was learned in later years. I know that we were commercializing Christmas too much now. I hope we can still let children learn the joy of giving and receiving during this special time of the year. Our Christ wants happiness and good will among all men and women. Also, he wants us to remember the Christmas Season of times past when we all greeted people with "Merry Christmas" and not "Happy Holidays". So with that thought I wish you a Merry Christmas and a Happy New Year!

Great Christmas memories of Goodwater include the lighting of the Christmas lights in downtown. I believe that was the most exciting night of the year in our little town. There were many colors glowing on the lines crossing Main Street. I remember the Alabama Power Company linemen putting the lights up under the direction of Mr. Hugh McClung and Mr. Joe 'Papa Joe' Worthy. Misters Speck, Max, Robert, Charles, Warner and others seemed to so enjoy their task of climbing those poles and hanging the lights. Usually, a big star of white lights was displayed in the middle of town but later years it was displayed on the building at the City Water Works on Goodwater Mountain. You could see it as far away as the three lane in Socapatoy. Goodwater was a busy place during this season. Great memories, great times past!

Next was an alley that went up the hill to the elementary school. If you entered the campus of Hilltop School you had to go up the hill from Weogufka Street or from another street they intersected with Brown St. If you approached Hilltop from Brown street the first house on the right was the Bud Gilliland house and directly across the street was the Duncan Brown house. In the next house on the side of the Bud Gilliland House was an old house that burned or just fell in and an old lady had lived in it. I was told that she was a witch. I doubt that but most kids thought that any old woman that lived alone was a witch. The next house was a big house that bordered the playground that the Sherum Family lived in at one time. I remember some of us kids went into the remains of the old house and found some decorations that had been a part of an old lamp or even an old necklace.

We all swore to secrecy as we divided up our new found jewels. There was a lot of melted glass and we thought that was jewels too. Does anyone remember that old house and its occupant? It was spooky! Below that was Brown's Grocery owned and operated by Duncan Brown and his sister. They lived in the big white house behind the store. I remember going there in the summer time and spending my five cent allowance. They had some candy as cheap as four for a penny. We really could do a lot of shopping with a nickel.

Next Was Chapman's Five and Dime store as they were called back then. Mr. Bertram (Doc) and Mrs. Gladys Chapman were owner operators and they were greatly assisted by Ms. Rebecca Chapman and their three children Bo, Betty Sue and David. Ms. Rebecca or "Becky" as we all knew her was there at all times and she always greeted you by your full name. The store was somewhat similar to today's Walmart. During the Christmas season the store was busy and all of the Chapman kids were on hand to help. It was so unique in Goodwater during this era that all you had to do to visit a schoolmate was to go to the next door store. This is where I bought my marbles, kites and Bolo paddles with the rubber ball attached by a long rubber band. The business was once on the east side of main street but in later years moved to the west side. The most prominent memory was that Becky was always so happy!

Now the lower one third of this side of the street is a little fuzzy in my memory! Next below Chapman's was Lawley Oil Company and the Pittsburgh Paint Store. I worked one summer for Mr. Jack and Fred Lawley and thoroughly enjoyed it. I had to work but the Lawley men were good men and treated everyone fair. I hated those oil deliveries though. A fifty-five gallon barrel of oil is heavy! Next door was a vacant store but I do remember an old truck being stored there. Later Mr. Barnett opened a TV and appliance repair store.

Then there was Herman Jacobs shoe store. Seems hard to believe in today's throw away world that you could get soles, half soles and heels replaced. He also carried a stock of shoes and usually had a gun or two for sale or trade.

Another barbershop was owned by Gene Shurette and it had a barber pole out front at one time. I can remember going in on Saturday mornings and having to wait for six or more people to get their hair cut. No appointments!

You always learned a lot in the barbershop! Sometimes there was a girlie magazine that had been left out and there was plenty of lying and scratching going on! Next was Mr. Walt Fomby's shoe store. Mr. Fomby had a good line of shoes that included the P.F. Flyers tennis shoe. Lord how they would stink! Rosemary McMahan remembers Mr. Fomby also sold jeans and work clothes as well as shoes. She also recalls the little western dolls that advertised Levi's. I believe Mrs. Fomby was a Canadian. I can remember her playing her violin in our Presbyterian Church a few times. I heard that she was a graduate of music from some well established college in New York.

Next down the road was E. Robinson Hardware that was owned by Ford Robinson and maybe Dot Holcomb. I think they may have been brother and sister. Mr. Bob Holcomb was always there as were the Strong Brothers and Bobbie Bruce.

It was always a treat to go to the hardware store as you could get anything from dinnerware to plows to tools and hardware. That store drew more people to Goodwater than any other business, I believe.

Another local store was Williamson's Grocery that was owned and operated by Mr. and Mrs. Williamson. I didn't know them well but I do remember Mr. Williamson had an elevated shoe on his right foot. I was too polite to ask why.

Later that business became a plumbing supply store and was owned and operated by Robert Culberson.

Next was Luker Truck and Tractor Store and Supply. The store was owned and operate by Mr. Horace and Mrs. Linnie Pearl Luker and they sold International Harvester Tractors and trucks. It seems that every Halloween their tractors appeared in the street. They had a good business as at one time the State of Alabama purchased most of their tractor parts from them.

Across the street was the Baptist Church and then you had Dr. H. L. Cockerham's office. You could get about anything on you fixed there. Dr. Cockerham was a great doctor and surgeon and I guess he knew everyone in Goodwater by name. He was always straight forward and always gentle. He had two women working for him, nurse Maddie Lou Burnette and June McCord his secretary who was a widow and they were always there. Last but not least there was the Goodwater Presbyterian Church.

Goodwater North

Crossing North over the overhead bridge or viaduct in Goodwater placed you in one of the most frequented places in town, 'The Dari Delite'. I remember its opening and it was hard to believe that we could get an ice cream cone with a twist at the top. We were finally really uptown. I think the first operator was Mr. McBride and we were so excited to have a place that stayed open past dark. It was a favorite for teenagers and was the place to hang out. We spent many hours sitting on the hoods of cars and visiting with each other. I'm sure that there had been trouble there but I don't recall any. I did see several transmissions become separated as boys would show out going up the hill toward the swimming pool and missing second gear. That was not good but still funny!

Continuing up the hill toward Ashland if your transmission was still in one piece was the Goodwater swimming pool and the American Legion 'Hut'. The swimming pool originated through a community project of the GW Lion's Club and stayed open several years. I think Jeff McCord, Sally McCord Sheehan's brother, was the first lifeguard. Jeff kept things under control as he was a big ole boy but more important everyone liked him. Mrs. Deon Neighbors taught swimming lessons several years and I'm here to tell you she was in charge while doing so!

She taught so many of us how to swim and I remember being a member of the swim team. We went to Clanton once for a swim meet and I don't think we won a single event other than springboard diving. The late Rickey Duke was fantastic on the spring board. Those folks in Chilton County had never seen anything to compare with him. He learned to dive out of a tree along the banks of Hatchet Creek and he was really good!

Heading back down toward the Dari Delite and turning left on the Brownville Road for about three miles and then turning right you were on the road to Spider Lake. Spider Lake was owned by Ms. Patti Fleming who was the Town Clerk. I remember fishing there several times. I later learned that others used it as a place for them and their sweetie to watch the moon! I never remember catching a fish out of the pond! I guess that was the reason it was free to fish!

Goodwater 280 South

Traveling down Highway 280 past the Goodwater Presbyterian Church for about a mile and a half we would be in front of Mr. Kirby Porter's small engine repair. Mr. Bill Dean, mail carrier and Robert Pate worked there. Robert Pate was a gentle giant that was so humble and nice. I always admired his humility and he didn't have to be humble! I remember going to an auction there when I was a toddler. Mr. Staten Tate ran a business there and I remember a tuba was going to be auctioned off and I wanted it so bad even though I couldn't play it or anything else!

Next down the road was Mr. Hugh McKelvey's gas station/store and it was opened all day on Sunday! Bad! Bad! Particularly at that time! 'Blue Laws' and all! Mr. Hugh carried me 'possum hunting once and we caught two that one night.

I later taught others a trick he taught me about carrying a 'possum out of the woods. He split a small hickory sapling with his axe and put the 'possum's tail in the split he had made in the hickory sapling and then removed the axe thus clamping tight on the opossum's tail. Worked like a charm.

Continuing on the trip was one of my favorites places to go. Dorman Robbin's Station Store. Mr. Robbins and his precious wife, Margie, owned and operated the store.

Dorman, as everyone called him, sold hunting equipment, turkey callers and even a dog if you were in the market for a good squirrel dog, a bird dog or even a duck dog! He was always jovial and I guess he knew everyone and opened very early! He always had time for the teenage boys to stop by and chew the fat. His two daughters, Leigh Robbins Barnett and Julia Robbins Bearden were GHS students and good Presbyterians! Of course, across the Road was Dixie Craft which I guess it was the largest employer in Coosa County. Mr. Walter Dowdle was the owner and operator and a real gentleman. He and his business helped Goodwater tremendously. Walter Jr. and Lynn, his children, were GHS students.

Next and across the road was a business I believe was Lynda's Dairy Bar. Mr. Charlie Sewell operated that business. Across the highway from Lynda's was Rogers Service Station owned and operated by Cliff and Leon Rogers. Scott Rogers was the primary operator. They sold gas, cokes and fishing equipment.

Fun place and they sold red worms for bait. Gwen, Joe, Scotty, Ann, Martha Ennis, Buddy and Noell were GHS students. Next but not least although it was small was 'The Pit'. A Bar-B-Que and hamburger business owned by Red Burns. It was a small building that was owned and operated by Red and the place where he cooked his Bar-B-Que and burgers. They were quiet tasty. I know he probably sold more burgers than McDonald's because I probably ate a million by myself! It was the only hamburger I have ever eaten where the condiments consisted only of Bar-B-Que sauce.

Traveling on the East side of Highway 280 past the National Guard Armory Mr. James 'Trigger' Dark was the owner/operator of Dark's Garage and Auto Parts. I am not sure when he built that new shop but it is still in operation by his grandson. 'Trigger', as all the grownups called him, had a wrecker and it was used a lot as the Highway Patrol called on him to get wrecked cars out of the way.

While both of his sons learned their trade from 'Trigger' the referee that kept things stable was his sweet wife Mrs. Ruth. She had her hands full but she could handle Mr. Dark, Paul and Glenn. She was quiet but had a special touch! Jerolyn, Martha, Bethy, Paul and Glenn were all GHS students. The Dark Family and auto repair was synonymous! Next was Tri-County Milling owned and operated by Mr. Morris and Billie Hawkins.

It was significant in the 1950-60s as a lot of people raised corn and needed it to be crushed for corn meal or cow feed! Mr. Billie and Morris were jovial people and had time for everyone that came by. Beth and Lynn were our age and were also GHS students.

Goodwater Hackneyville Street

If your turned right (east) at the lower red light in town you were on Hackneyville Street. Prior to crossing the rail road there was a street that ran parallel with the rail road. It was aptly named Railroad Street! On this street was The McCord Oil Company that was owned and operated by George McCord, Sally McCord Sheehan's father. Mr. McCord was always a happy fellow and he knew all of us boys by our first name. He always had something to say to us and it was always a joy to see and visit with him. Mr. Jake Richardson sort of ran things and was always at work early, very early!

Mr. S.O."Shine" Buzbee, who worked for Lawley Oil Co. had a nickname for everyone. He called me 'Joe Palooka', Mr. Fred Lawley he called 'Big Captain', Mr. Jack Lawley he called 'Top Man' and he even called a lady with no teeth 'Smooth Mouth'!

If you turned right before crossing the rail road there was Sterling Lumber and Supply and it employed several dozen men. Mr. Charles F. Thomas was the last owner. Mr. John L. Davidson was the man in charge. They sold wood pallets, wood boxes and lumber. Sterling lost a big building one spring to a fire and it made a mess. Black ash was about two feet deep!

Mr. Thomas hired me and an African-American kid to clean it up. The other black kids would laugh at me and tell me that they could not tell me from the other young fellow that was helping. We were both black as smut! I had to wash off at an outside spigot when I got home in the afternoon. Continuing on the main road about a mile and a half out of town was Mr. Walter Barber's Store located at Double Bridges.

I remember they had a kitchen in the back of the store where Mrs. Barber cooked lunch and supper. They were the parents of Donnie and Donna who were both GHS students. Mr. Barber was a quiet and friendly man.

Goodwater Weogufka Street

I never did understand the reason for the name of that street. Luker Truck and Tractor and the Baptist Church occupied the corners and the next building on the right was our new U.S. Post Office with a circular drive. Mr. L.L. Buttram was the Postmaster and was well respected by everyone.

He even fixed TVs. His two daughters, Rose and Mary, were GHS Students. Mary and I were at Auburn at the same time. I started a year before Mary but we finished at the same time! Later the new Goodwater Library was built next to the post office.

Next up we had a new Alabama Power Company (APC) building. It was owned by Mr. Griffin Harris. The APC office stayed open for many years but has recently closed. Mrs. Ruby Hickey handled business there for years and has recently retired. Ruby knew everybody in Goodwater and was so valuable to the APC.

Just across the street Robert (Bob) Hammond built Goodwater's first modern Super Market and it was called Bob's IGA. I remember when he would send weekly circulars advertising his specials. I thought we were in Birmingham!

In order to gain access to the next business you had to enter through the IGA parking lot. Danielle Browning Moody owned and operated a beauty shop. Everybody called her 'Mrs. Billie'. It seemed that five or six customer cars were there at all times. I worked in the IGA for several months and I got to see all that entered her shop! Ladies came from far around and even from Alexander City and I have to admit that they looked a lot better leaving than they did when they arrived!

I believe I am correct when I remember a lady driving too close to the shop and then hit it! The lady got out of her car and wanted to know who was at fault. Go figure!

Good or Bad! Coosa County and Goodwater had been 'dry' forever. I remember Bob Hammond leading the cause to get the county to vote 'wet'. I had my doubts as there were still a lot of 'bootleggers' and they were against it as were the preachers!

I remember the day after the referendum I was in Auburn eating breakfast at Klinner's (The Ditch) and picked up a Birmingham News and was scanning it when I came upon the article about Coosa County going 'wet'. I was rather surprised at the outcome! That was in my school year 1967-68! A little later Kellyton became the busiest place in Coosa County as Tallapoosa county was still 'dry'. The county line stores had customers parking all along U.S. Highway 280!

This about winds up my short and quick journey through Goodwater. I can feel and see so many of the things I mentioned in my mind. I can tell that there are a lot of you all that still love and enjoy those times of many years ago. Goodwater was and will always be in our memories and in our hearts. I enjoyed sharing my confused memories and I hope that we can now share memories of some people that made Goodwater a great place.

Family Gatherings

When I was a small boy back in the mid-to-late 1950s, our family would always gather at my grandparent's home for Thanksgiving and Christmas on 'The Old Dark Road' in Alex City. One thing I always looked forward to at these family gatherings was the great meal we would all share. My Mom would cook her specialties as did her sisters, her brother's wives and of course my grandmother's famous fried chicken and homemade rolls. There were no frozen casseroles, no 'Hamburger Helper' and NO 'Colonel's Chicken'.

When it was time to eat my Uncle Howell Britton would always say grace and thank the good Lord for all the blessings that He had bestowed upon us. Part of his prayer was meant to remind us of how fortunate we were to be a family. The men would then get a plate and meander through all those great foods. Next were the women. Our Moms usually held two or more plates. One for them and one for their children. Judy Harris Cooper says she the women still get two plates at her reunions for the same reason. One for the kids and for themselves! Everyone had something to eat and was filled to the point of exploding and there was usually plenty left. No person was left wanting.

After everyone had finished the meal the men would gather to talk business, politics or local community issues. The women would all gather and talk about the latest fashions, church 'doin's' or whatever women talk about. The kids would run around outside like wild Indians and try to get the best of our cousins. At the end of the day we were all tired, but it was a wonderful feeling. Those were some great times. Nowadays, it seems the kids demand to be the first in line for the meal and could care less about playing outside and just want to get back home to get on the internet or play a game on their X-Box or PlayStation.

Donna Ledbetter reminded me how things have sure changed in our lifetime. She remembers hearing her parents talk about how life was so simple when they were young. She says she never understood what they meant until she got a few years under her belt. Life indeed was much more relaxed in years past. Today we have to hurry up and get somewhere and do something. No time to slow down and get back to our upbringings.

Ed Cook says he can relate 100% to that. He reports that at his last gathering or reunion there were no children at all. The reunion was just all adults and after lunch people began leaving. Seems not many were interested in the family history research that he had brought. Ed says he mentioned this to a co-worker and she said their reunions last all weekend with food, games and shopping. Ed lamented that his reunions last about three hours at best and like Robert said, everyone seems to be in too big a hurry these days.

Very sad what we have lost. Unfortunately, we can only remember those great times in our memories. I re-live many of them even to this day. When we are gone, our memories of a more simple life will be forever forgotten. If only we had a magic recorder of days gone by in order to be able to share with our children and their children. Alas, our histories are but a small grain of sand that will be washed away into the vast ocean of life. RD

The Photo

This is the last photo I have of the house that my Grannie and Grandfather lived in and that I learned about cooking, life and that things do not always go your way. It's called life. For most folks it is just a picture of an old house that is about ready to fall in. For the record I am the guy in the photo. To me it is NOT just a house, it is my life and memories and it is a shame it has come to this. Where you see the tree that covers the left side of the house is where the chimney was. It had fallen down by this time and someone had came and took the bricks. Why I don't know. I would love to have just one of those. There was a space of about an inch or so between the house and the chimney which would let the winter winds in like nobody's business. That is why we had to do the 'fireplace dance' to try to stay warm. You can't see that in the photo but it is there.

The front porch roof has fallen down and is on the verge of collapsing but that is where my grandfather would nap on his hammock in the heat of the afternoon. We also sat on that porch and listened to the bobwhites and whip-o-wills in the evening after supper. My sister from Hell was a baby and the folks had put some tar on the roof to fix some leaks and she had stepped in it. My Grandfather pressed her foot onto a board under there and the imprint is still there to this day. You can't see that in the photo but it is there. This is also the porch where an old misty eyed woman stood and watched her Marine grandson go off to fight in a war she didn't quite understand, not knowing if she would ever see him alive again. You can't see that in the photo but it is there.

Under the porch is where I played and lived lives beyond the imagination of anyone who has never experienced the wonders of being under a porch and young. Doodlebugs, aliens, pirates, spaceships and other things that my part timers will not let me remember. You can't see that in the photo but it is there. The old tin roof is starting to go. This is the same roof that our neighbors came and helped replace after a storm tore the old one off. They did this to help out some old people that could never repay them for their kindness. But that is the way it was back then. I miss those times. You can't see that in the photo but it is there. On the right side hidden by the house is where the well was. This is where we (read I) drew water for drinking, washing, cooking, etc. until it went dry that one time. You can't see that in the photo but it is there.

In front of the house where I am standing is the road that went through the yard. The old walnut tree is on the other side of the road. The road is where we played and the tree is what we climbed. We caught leaves falling from it and sat under it and peeled peaches under it and such. That's where the wash house was. You can't see that in the photo but it is there. Behind the house is the pecan tree and next to that are the fig trees. We ate of their bounty many times. Also, an old smokehouse was back there where we cured and dried the meat from the hogs that we would butcher. You can't see that in the photo but it is there. When people die there is a ceremony and such and a headstone and all but when an old house dies no one seems to notice until they come around later and it is no longer there or in disrepair. At least I have this photo. It is a monument to my life and that of my youth. It is who I am! You can't see that in the photo either but it is there! PGG

Saying Goodbye

I went to a former Goodwater High School (GHS) graduate's funeral this week. It was a sorrowful day for such a young man to die. He was only sixty-six! Steve graduated GHS in 1965. I was sad and proud. Sad for the death of my friend. I was proud because of the men and women that were there that had graduated from GHS. The women are always pretty and their beauty speaks for itself both inward and outward. The men were all well groomed and all were dressed to represent a southern gentleman paying his respects. I grew up knowing all those older folks that were young once and were schoolmates of mine and seeing how they presented themselves. It made me proud and it made me cry! They all conducted themselves in such a honorable and respectful way that would have even made Mr. Westbrook happy. Maybe a lot happier than his annual 'White Christmas'! If you didn't go to GHS you don't know about that 'White Christmas'.

Steve and I fought almost everyday at football practice. We pushed, punched and shoved every play and I laughed and he always had that Gillum giggle. Steve had that laugh as did Tommy and Don. Never mad. He had that shuffle when you walked. Guess you had to see it. We need to visit our old friends more. I'm sure there were a lot of good schools back then but there was none like ours. You see old schoolmates now and it just adds perk to your step and a warmth to your heart.

Steve Gillum was a good kid, young man and grown man. Above all he loved Jesus Christ and was a devoted member to his church. He was us, he was GHS. James Long the preacher that conducted his service is also one of us. Burying our own I guess! CL

Tommy adds the following. Would you believe I was just starting to write something about Steve when I saw your note. You listened to our English teacher a lot better than I did so it was better that you wrote the story. I was in total shock when I heard the news. Steve and I were best friends at GHS. I was at his home many times and he at mine back when we were in GHS. We had many good times from 1962-1965. About four years ago Steve, Bobby Ryals and Steve Lewis and I met at Cecil's for a mini reunion. We spent four hours that night talking about old times we had going to GHS. It had been over forty-four years since I had seen or talked to him. What a great night that was. They told some things on me that I did not remember and some I longed to forget!

This past March Steve came to visit me at my home. He met my wife for the first time and she really liked him but then again who didn't? He stayed for about two hours and again we talked old times. He was so positive about life and how he had found God. I was so happy for him. He looked great and said he felt good. He looked almost the same as when we left GHS. He gave me his cell number and told me to please call him and let's get together. I wish now I would have make that call.

I did go to the funeral home Sunday night and ran into many of our classmates. I had an emergency Monday and could not attend his funeral which made me really feel bad. Men like Steve Gillum do not come along too often in life. He is only the second one we have lost in our class in the forty-eight years since we left GHS. He will be greatly missed by anyone who ever knew him. I wish I had taken some pictures when Steve came for a visit. Maybe a donation to The American Heart Association in his memory would make me feel better.

Steve is buried at Hatchett Creek Presbyterian Church.

The Gliding Ghost of Goodwater

I first met Charles Harris when I came to Goodwater High School (GHS) from Kellyton in the 10th grade. Kellyton, being a Jr. High school, only had nine grades so we had to ride the bus to Goodwater. I remember him as a nice, quiet, good looking young man and a little bit mischievous, as we will find in a bit.

I remember one incident when Dan (the custodians') mule wound up in Mrs. Swindall's cloak room! Not calling any names but a few that could possibly have been involved were Charles, Buddy Rogers, Jerry Swindall, Joe Hardman, John Fulton, Chick McCord and others. Needless to say, there was quite a disturbance for a few minutes when she walked in and found that mule looking her in the face. I don't know who got out of there first, Mrs.Swindall or the mule!

The school year of 1948 some of the to be senior boys were held back and Charles was one of them. I graduated in May of 1949 and I never saw Charles after that. I married and began my family and Charles went on with his life. In spite of his academic set back he entered The University of Georgia (UG) in 1950. He went there to earn a degree and play football!

This was before high tech sports equipment came along. There was a tight, funny looking helmet, a few pads and high top shoes! This was way before Herschel Walker and Vince Dooley. Wally Butts was the head coach and he was hoping that quarterback Charlie Harris would help bring football and the Bulldogs back alive at UG. Charles was quick and fast and as he came from Goodwater he gained the name ' The Gliding Ghost of Goodwater' and we claimed him as one of our own! He had an excellent career, never equal to Walker's, but good. He was also captain of the track team.

With the U.S. involvement in the Korean War and Charles volunteering for three years in the Marines it took him seven years to complete his four year degree. He played football at Camp Pendleton, Ca. They were highly motivated to succeed because if they were dropped from the team they found themselves in Korea.

After the Marines he played on the UG teams of 1954-56 and had a brief stint with the New York Titans and made it to the final cut for the Cleveland Browns. He later became a high school coach at Newnan High School in Georgia. This is where he taught Lewis Grizzard's health class. Lewis later wrote about Charles in his book, *Don't Sit Under The Grits Tree With Anyone Else But Me* and spoke highly of him. This is a special tribute for any teacher to receive from a former pupil.   During the days of Hershel Walker's breaking all records, Charles was fighting his own battle. He had been diagnosed with Leukemia. Charles was still a long distance runner at age forty-nine long before being a runner became popular. A run of twenty miles was nothing for him. He ran in the inaugural Peachtree Road Race. He had reached the point however that his endurance was waning. He was still going by what he had learned under Coach Wally Butts and that was to try to run it out. It wasn't working anymore! Charles told Lewis on a visit late in his life that what he learned from all this is that no one is indestructible. No one!

It still brings a lump to my throat when I think of all the good times we shared and a life taken way too soon. Charles was a husband, father, high school principal, church man and never drank or smoked. Dr. Charles Harris died in the spring of 1981. He left behind a wife and three children. Well done good and faithful servant! Rebecca Shivers.

This is something that I wrote nearly two years ago when one of my best friends, Rose Buttram Graham, passed away. Although it was inspired by Rose's passing, it is really in a lot of ways just as much about the kind of childhood that we all had in Goodwater and the sadness/nostalgia that we feel as we realize that it has passed and that the little town that we loved is no longer as it was. This could be about so many others, not just Rose.

Losing Rose

A big part of my happy childhood came to an end last night when I learned of the death of one of my very best childhood friends. Growing up in a small Alabama community, all of us knew everybody in town, so we had a wide group of friends. With only forty or so in our class, which was the largest Goodwater ever had, we were close not only to those in our class but also to those who were two or three years ahead of us and those who were two or three years behind us. Our birthday parties generally had six or seven years worth of children playing happily together.

While I claimed to have quite a few really good friends, I really had only two very best friends, Rose and Sandra. They were both in my class from first grade until graduation and we had many sleep overs, 4-H camp trips, club conventions and all that sort of thing and their parents sort of adopted me, an only child, after my father died suddenly of a heart attack when I was just thirteen.

The Thomas's hosted me many week-ends at their cabin on Lake Martin. It was Sandra's daddy who taught me how to water ski. It was Rose's daddy who let me ride with their family to all the out-of-town football games since Mama didn't want to drive on those little country roads at night with just the two of us. Both of their mothers were wonderful cooks and I can still remember some of the aromas that emanated from their kitchens on my frequent sleep-overs at both of their houses.

Rose and I were such close friends in elementary school that one year we convinced the school photographer to take our picture together, as he did for our classmates Mary and Myra Rush, who were twins. Somehow I lost this relic but at our last reunion Rose brought one as part of our memorabilia.

I do have a copy of a group class picture from the second or third grade where we stood next to each other on the back row with our arms crossed across each others shoulder.

After high school graduation, we all sort of drifted apart but our parents remained close, so we were able to keep up to some extent with what the others were doing. Then, as often happens, as each of us approached our retirement years we re-connected when we began working on a couple of class reunions.

At that time Rose and Sandra were living in Montgomery and I was living in Auburn, so we were close enough to get together for lunch and to make plans for our class' 50th reunion, which was in April of 2011. Rose, Sandra and I divided our class roster, which by then was down to twenty-seven or so, giving each of us less than ten to contact. Then we would call each other and meet again, going up to Five Star Plantation, where our reunion was held. Occasionally we would have lunch at Carlisle's Drugstore in Alex City or meet in Montgomery for lunch at Sinclair's and as always sharing memories of things we had done more than half a century ago.

After the reunion, we continued to talk on the phone and we tried to get Rose to come to some of the multi-class 'Goodwater Girls' get togethers that we had begun having three or four times a year. Sandra and I broke our necks to be there. I remember I showed up once on a walker with a broken pelvis but Rose didn't come. Looking back now, I think she was too weak and ill to attend but she didn't want us to know.

She had been seriously ill for six months but she wouldn't let her sister Mary tell us. Maybe it's just as well. She had a lot of pride and didn't want us to see her declining before our eyes. Now I can look back on that last, happy evening we had together at our fiftieth reunion. Rose and Jim, Sandra and Jerry, Betty and John, all at the same table at the reunion with our old classmates. We were laughing and sharing hilarious stories from those 'Happy Days' much like the sit-com set in that era! A time when we could walk all over town with no fear and we would spend lazy afternoons sipping cherry cokes at Audie Holmes' drug store. The worst thing we could do was to be in a convertible with some guys who shot out a city street light with a BB gun on Halloween and get hauled down to the Goodwater Police Station. Rose and I got to sit in the car and Mr. Buttram went over to my house to explain to Mama what had happened.

The boys had to pay for the broken street light and even those which others had destroyed but were not caught and charged.

Today I'm just sad. Sad that Rose is gone, sad that my little town has gone and sad that one of the most important parts of my childhood has gone. BDB

And of course Clyde!

I got Clyde settled in the Goodwater Nursing Home as well as you could settle Clyde. Mrs. Margie (Leigh Robbins Barnett) was working at the nursing home and she was just like my mama. I had known her all of my life as we went to the same church for years. She was a best friend of our family and especially my mother. When I went to the nursing home she was almost laughing at my predicament with Clyde. I went to see Clyde several times over the next few weeks he lived there and I could tell he wasn't the happiest camper in the tent. It was winter time and it was cold outside but Clyde's room was seventy-six degrees, the floor was clean and Clyde was clean. He was getting as fat as a yard dog and he had a mouth full of snuff but nowhere to spit! He told me he wanted me to carry him home but I told him he wasn't quiet ready to go yet! Then right after the first of the month I was working in the courthouse and I was told I had a phone call I needed to take. It was Mrs. Margie with the news that Clyde had escaped and couldn't be found. I told her I would be there in a few minutes so I headed out to search for Clyde!

Upon my arrival I was greeted by Mrs. Margie and she told me that the police had found Clyde on the Hackneyville Road standing in the middle of a kudzu patch. It was several miles from the nursing home so he was serious about leaving. The police persuaded Clyde to return to the nursing home until they could get things settled. Mrs. Robbins told me that when they had presented him his Social Security check to sign to give to the nursing home to help in paying for his room and board he became belligerent. He would not let them have it back and I guess as they were discussing a method to get the check back he left.

I went to Clyde's room and asked him how he was doing and his response was short! "I want to go home!" I told him to hang on a few minutes and let me see if I could work something out and told him not to leave! I went to Mrs. Margie's office and told her our predicament was hopeless.

I told her that he had lived a rough, cold, dirty, hard life. He had lived with a mouth full of snuff all of his life and he was not going to adjust to this lifestyle! I told her the best thing for all involved was for me to take Clyde home and let him die in peace. She agreed!

I went back to Clyde's room and asked if he was ready to go home and he smiled and jumped out of his chair ready to go. I got a couple of paper grocery bags and packed his belongings in them and he beat me to my car! I stopped at the Piggly Wiggly and bought Clyde several pounds of bananas, a half-gallon of milk, some crackers, Vienna sausages, potted meat and several more staple items! So off we went to Keyno and Clyde's homecoming. I noticed while unloading him and his food he was the happiest man I think I have ever seen. I rounded up a pickup load of firewood for him and he was set. He could wait for God in leisure and comfort and most important in his own home!

Clyde got a little better and was trying to get me to plow up a field for him to plant some watermelons and I told him that I would knowing that he would never see the first one sprout. He had several more bouts of various illnesses over the next few months and could just never shake it off. One day when I got home from work I did not see Clyde out and about. I was informed that Clyde had gone to live with his sister, Polly, in Alex City. The rascal didn't even say goodbye! After a few weeks I was told that Clyde had had a spell and was in Russell Hospital. In a day or two I was futher informed that Clyde had died. I went to his graveside funeral at the church on Coosa County Road 42 and actually shed a tear or two. Not so much for missing him but knowing a man who went through a long hard life and never experienced the joy of love, the love of children or a place to call home except for one place. I am thankful that Melinda and I didn't take that one home away. Maybe, just maybe, Clyde will let me live just behind his cabin in Glory Land! CL

Passings

Tommy reminisces that his Dad passed away twenty-six
years ago today. He would have been ninety-nine years old. He was
born Nov. 7th 1915. The picture is my Dad Drew and Mother Annie
Lynn that was taken in the summer of 1967. My Dad was only age
fifty-one in this picture and my Mother was forty-nine yet they
seemed much older to me back then. It seems like it was only
yesterday. As people pass so do small towns.

Pamela Kellogg reported the following after she drove
through the town or what is left of it. My goodness it is in sad sad
shape. My family grocery store and drug store are gone and most of
the buildings on the right side of street are falling down. My heart
was broken looking at this little town where we all had the best time
playing, going to school and church. The town may not be the same
but the memories in my heart will always be of our lazy little town
where we all had a great childhood and so much love.

Tommy says he drove through Goodwater a few months ago
and saw the same things she did. It was such a great town back in the
1950s and 1960s and then it went down quick. Not sure why but it
happened. I wish now I had not made the tour because I wanted to
remember it like we all did back in the good old Goodwater High
School days. We still have the good memories of those days that I
hope nobody can ever take away.

Charlotte Shivers took the picture of my folks here as she
traveled to Texas with my parents to bring my car to me. I had been
in Guam for six months and badly needed the car. What a blast we
all had in Amarillo the few days they all spent with me. Charlotte
says they were like her second mom and dad and she still misses
them so much.

Gwen Payne Qualizza shares a memory she'll never forget of
her Uncle Drew getting in the floor and helping her lay out the fabric
and pattern for a dress she was making. She has kept the dress all
these years! What a sweet memory it brings back!

Bethy Trout recalls that Tommy's Daddy was such a great
champion of humor! So true of all the Dark boys I've known and
even those descendants of Jim and Annie four generations down the
road! Maybe God created a gene for humor and wit in the DNA. My
family loved spending Christmas Eve with yours but we couldn't
wait for you guys to leave so Santa Claus could hurry up and come!
You always got a new Timex watch every year, as I remember!

Tommy says he remembers the Timex watches. Wonders what he did with them? I know every year I was threatened with a bag of switches Something people today probably never hear at Christmas!

Betty DeGraffenried Burgess sadly says that she doesn't think Goodwater was ever truly beautiful/picturesque the way some other small towns may be! The true beauty was in the hearts of those who lived there. However, today it's just sad to see the buildings falling down in disrepair. Our house was leveled a number of years ago after the people who purchased it from Mama abandoned it. It breaks my heart to see the whole town falling to pieces. People pass, towns pass, we pass!

James Long and The 'Fessor

Life was good in Hanover. Any time you can buy a Coke and a Baby Ruth candy bar for five cents each life has got to be good. You could get your necessities at any corner of the community, Bailey's or Darden's on the southern end and Hule Reynold's on the northern. If you were so inclined and went east there was Albert and Evelyn Smith's store.

One thing that I remember is that everyone was your neighbor. There weren't all that many people around but everyone would extend a helping hand. People were good and doors were never locked. We kids were just having a good time being with one another. At sunset we wanted to stay a little longer like the next moment was holding something special and we would miss that moment if any of us went home. The boys were always playing marbles, baseball, basketball or playing cowboys and Indians with stick guns and horses. Everybody wanted to be Roy Rogers.

Our mothers always reminded us boys "no playing marbles for keeps"! We didn't listen. Earl Lambert and my brother, George, were the marble champions. At least their marble bags were always full and the others about empty.

Sammy Cunard was Mr. Football. He could kick a football to the moon and back. We would make a ball of old socks with a rock inside, grab an old limb and the baseball game was about to begin and even flies and scooters. But our favorite game was basketball. Mr. Archie Dobson was the principal and basketball coach. He would often open the school gym on Saturdays so we boys could play. Mr. Dobson was a special man and loved by all. All the boys called him by his nickname, 'Fessor.

The girls were always busy doing whatever girls do. My two older sisters, Delia Faye and Betty, often stayed in their rooms to listen to the radio. On a Saturday night I could hear The Grand Ole Opry coming from the side room which was their bedroom. How long has it been since someone used the term 'side room'?

Katydids are another term that people don't use much anymore. Kids don't even know what they are. And what about Doodlebugs? At other times I could stand outside their room and hear Joe Rumore spinning their favorite record from Birmingham. That new singer, the one with the swivel hips and the funny name which I couldn't remember, would sing the words "love me tender, love me true, all my dreams fulfill. For my Darling, I love you and I always will" I still can't understand why all those girls were so crazy about him.

The winters were cold and the summers were hot with no air conditioning anywhere. Of course, most had running water which was the spring that was running behind the house. We would run to the spring with a bucket in hand. Wash pots, scrub boards, lye soap and elbow grease cleaned everyone's overalls for church on Sunday. Some Sundays there was even fried chicken. Momma would catch a young pullet, wring it's neck, clean it, cut it up and fry it in an old black cast iron frying pan full of hog lard. Homemade hot biscuits, fried chicken and cold buttermilk for lunch. Wow!

The boys would always have a swimming hole which they made by taking rocks and building a dam in a small stream. Other times Momma would set a wash tub in the sun and by three in the afternoon the water would be just right for three kids and a hound dog. After a summer rain, the boys would get an old tin can, fill it with worms and go fishing for mud cats. "You take a wiggly worm, watch him squirm, put him on a hook and drop him in a brook. If everything goes right, we'll fry fish tonight. Country boy ain't got no shoes, Country boy ain't got no blues." just as Johnny Cash sang it in his song "Country Boy". We were all just barefoot country boys. We would be considered as living in poverty, but we were rich in love. The love of family, friends, neighbors and our teachers as well.

There were always boys at our house. I always thought they were there because they liked my brother George and me. Then I realized that they didn't want to play marbles anymore. They wanted to hang out with our sisters. I wondered why?

The Culberson family lived just below us and Morris 'Mo' always rolled an old used tire everywhere he went. I always wanted one of those tires to roll but never could afford one! The Culbersons had the only TV set in the community. Roy Rogers gave way to Davy Crockett. Walt Disney was king. Mo would give us the okay to come on down to eat a tater sandwich and watch Davy Crockett on Saturday night. I always wanted a coon skin cap but never got one of those either. However, when I preached this sermon at Sycamore United Methodist Church about a year ago one of the ladies had a gift bag for me the very next Sunday. I finally had my coon skin cap. I looked so good in it I preached for a minute or two wearing that thing!

I was thirteen years old and had never had any experience with death but it came to our house anyway. It took my mother with a heart attack. My sister, Betty and I were alone with her that morning. We held her in our arms and cried as passed over to be with Jesus. All those good times were about be memories as we would have to move away from our little hometown of Hanover.

My mother was buried at Andrew's Chapel United Methodist Church cemetery in Hanover. The though of moving away was tearing me up. I had never been farther out of Hanover than to Tallassee for a family reunion each year. We went to Rockford about four times a year for a twenty-five cent haircut. Every friend I had in the world was in Hanover. I did not want to leave. The preacher had said his final amen at the grave site and the grownups were giving their condolences to the older family members. I was the youngest. I was more or less forgotten or so I thought. From out of nowhere I felt a big loving arm come around my shoulder. I looked up and saw that it was Mr. Dobson. It was 'Fessor's arm. He said, "Jim (he always called me Jim) come and let's walk together." We walked back across the road to the church yard and say down on the roots of a big old oak tree. He began to talk to me about life and death. I cried and he wiped tears from his eyes as well. He tried to make me feel better about myself by saying, "Jim, we don't want to lose you. We need you on the basketball team." Hanover had won the county tournament in 1957 but that's another story. My sister, Delia Faye, had also won the county spelling bee. Mr. Dobson also told me he loved me. He loved every child he had ever taught. However, it was already decided that we would be moving to Kellyton.

The school year had already begun and I had entered eighth grade at Hanover but I would be attending Kellyton now. Something special happened at Kellyton, I was accepted by everyone! I love those Kellyton folks and always will. It seemed like every kid in the school went out of their way to welcome me and make me feel at home. Mr. James Floyd and Mr. Lloyd McCellen were two special teachers and Mr. McCellen was also the basketball coach. He took me to the gym and said, "Hit five out of ten free throws." I made seven out of ten. Kellyton would win the county basketball tournament that year of 1961. The ninth grade had about eight boys that were all good players; Robert "Butch' Dark, Tommy Dark, Larry Shivers, Mike Ogburn, Steve Lewis, Gary Shivers, Perry Richardson, Bobby Flournoy and others. I fell in love with the other eighth grade boys and we became the "B" team.

Kellyton's first game that year was against none other than Hanover! I would get to play against my old buddy, Larry Carden or so I thought. 'Fessor had moved him up to the "A" team. The game was played at Kellyton. We came out to warm up and I saw some of my old friends on the other end of the court. I also saw 'Fessor. We were shooting practice shots and all at once I felt a familiar loving arm slip around my shoulder. It belonged to 'Fessor. He asked how I was doing? More small talk and then he said, "Jim, we still love you at Hanover and by the way, you're wearing the wrong color jersey!" He gave me a big bear hug and said, "Jim, play your best." I cried. The first half Hanover led all the way. The second half was no different.

With about three minutes left in the game and Hanover ahead by four points Mr. McCellen called time out and we huddled up. He gave us our instructions, "We must play defense. We can't give up any more points and expect to win. When we get the ball nobody is to shoot but James! Feed him the ball and let him take the shot." We did play defense and Hanover didn't score any more points. My teammates fed me the ball and I got lucky and made three baskets with the last one just a few seconds before the final second ticked off the clock. Kellyton had won the game with their only lead of the night! The crowd went wild! The cheerleaders ran out onto the court. We huddled up and were shouting and jumping around.

Then out of nowhere I felt an ole loving arm slip around my shoulder again. 'Fessor was the first to say, "Good game." He told me once again that I was wearing the wrong color jersey and that he loved me. He would also stop worrying about me as I was now in good hands. One last hug and he walked back to his team.

Even as he suffered the pain of the loss he was telling me how much he loved me. Even in his agony he was telling me I would always be one of his children, one of his boys. I believe that we all know another man like that. That man is Jesus. As he suffered on the cross he was saying, "I love you." As he hung there in agony he was telling us, "You're someone special, you're worth my dying for!" Jesus also said, "When you've done it for the least of these, you've also done it for me. " Matthew 25:40

Times were much simpler and less complicated back then. You knew your neighbors by name and everyone was willing to pitch in and lend a helping hand. Everyone was willing to slip their arm around someone in need and say, "I love you." Just an eighth grade basketball game but the memory of that night will forever be etched in my mind and heart just as all those good friends and days from Hanover. Just as 'Fessor's memory will never die. It is alive and well today in the hearts of all 'his kids'! Maybe we need to give our arms a workout. Maybe, just maybe, God will put someone in our path that needs a hug from one of His children. Maybe that someone will be you. Slip your arm around someone when you are given the opportunity. May the good Lord bless and keep you. In the name of Jesus. Amen.

Robert P. 'Butch' Dark Jr.

I was born July 12, 1947 and raised in Kellyton, Alabama. My father ran an auto mechanics business in Goodwater and started taking me to his shop at the ripe old age of eight. It was my job to sweep the floor, clean engine parts and keep all Dad's tools in their proper place. I rebuilt my first engine (lawn mower) at age twelve and painted my first vehicle at age fourteen. I attended Kellyton Jr. High then transferred to Goodwater for grades ten and eleven. I graduated from BRHS in Alex City in 1965. I continued working for my father for a while after high school and then did auto body repair for the State Highway Department at the old Highway Department and Convict Camp in Alexander City until I left for the USAF in 1966 and trained in Munitions Maintenance. I then earned a B.S. Degree in Vocational and Technical Education from Athens State University and eventually retired from teaching at Gadsden State Community College. I currently reside in Oxford, Alabama with my wife Patti. My parents taught me Christian values and how to treat my fellow man. I still live by their teachings today. I did not, however, fully grow into a self-disciplined man until I had the opportunity to spend over seven years in the United States Air Force.

Charles Luker

Charles L. Luker, was born in September 1949 and was
raised and educated in Goodwater, Alabama. He is a graduate of
Goodwater High School and attended Auburn University and
graduated in 1972. He is the only son of Mr. and Mrs. L.L. Luker
and he has two sisters, Mary Cathryn and Martha Jean. Charles was
adventurous and had a love for the outdoors and especially the
woods of Coosa County, Hatchet Creek, Weogufka Creek, Coosa
River and Lake Martin and loved to hunt and fish with his close
friends. He loved to visit old folks and hear their many stories of
times past. He loves his hometown of Goodwater and he feels it was
the greatest place on earth to grow up. The whole community was
close knit and he knew he was subject to being disciplined at every
turn. He knew all the folks and they all knew him but that was the
same with every child in Goodwater. His life greatly changed in
1978 when he ran for the countywide public office of Tax Assessor
and was elected. After serving six years he became Revenue
Commissioner and served in that position for the next twenty-seven
years. The thirty-four continuous years of service is the longest
for any official in Coosa County. After retirement Charles started
writing short stories of his experiences for his friends and many
encouraged him to publish those stories. So, here they are and they
are real but some names have been changed to protect the guilty. He
currently lives in Keno near Goodwater with his wife Melinda.

Tommy Dark

I was born August 22, 1947 in Kellyton Al just a few miles south of Goodwater. I went to Kellyton Jr. High until 1962 and then to Goodwater High School in the 10th grade where I graduated in 1965. My parents were sort of hard on me but I was a rebel so it never did much good. I worked for my dad in the summers until the one time I thought I wanted to try something else. I went to work for Coosa County using a bush ax clearing roadside brush which made me decide real quick I needed to get back into the shop. After graduating high school I attended Jacksonville State for two semesters in late 1965 and part of 1966. I then dropped out for a while and faced the draft. I did not want to go in the Army so I joined the USAF in 1966 and served four years. I got out in November 1970 then married my wife Jill, a girl I met while at my last duty station in Michigan. We married December seventh so I wouldn't forget my anniversary! We came home to Alabama and I went to work for my dad again and worked for him until I bought the business in 1979. I operated the garage under the new name of Dark's Garage until July 1997. I then closed it up and took a job at the Alex City golf course as the mechanic. I retired as the assistant superintendent in Feb 2012. Currently living in Alexander City and enjoying grandkids and playing golf!

Betty DeGraffenried Burgess

I was born October 5, 1943, in Montgomery, Alabama. My middle name is Thomas and I was called "Betty Thomas" for quite a while as I was growing up. When I was four, we moved to Goodwater to live with my grandfather as my grandmother had died. I graduated from Goodwater High School in 1961 and then attended Auburn University, graduating in 1965. Following in my mother's footsteps, I then taught English in Pensacola and Huntsville. I returned to Auburn for graduate school and received my master's degree in 1971 and my doctorate in English Education in 1974. I married John Burgess, Jr. on St. Patrick's Day in 1973 and have two children, Elizabeth and John III, both of whom now live in Birmingham. In 1982, I began working as an English teacher at Auburn High School, retiring in 2001 after an auto accident which required immediate surgery on my knee and eventually a total hip replacement. Fortunately, I recovered nicely and have said that I would like to write a "thank-you note" to the girl who hit me head-on since retirement is the job I was born to have! I retired from teaching English at Auburn High School in 2001. I now enjoy playing bridge, reading for pleasure, traveling, having lunch out with my friends, attending AU athletic events and sleeping late every morning. I also enjoy writing occasional articles for *The Auburn Villager.*

James W. Long

James W. Long was born on June 1, 1948 near Hanover in Coosa County, Alabama. He attended school at Hanover, Kellyton Junior High and graduated from Goodwater High School in 1966. He attended Alexander City State Junior College, now known as Central Alabama Community College, while working full time at Russell Corp. James joined the Air Force in 1968, served as a medic and was honorably discharged in 1971 after serving in Panama City, Florida and Ankara, Turkey. He married the former Dian Voss from Alexander City in 1968 and they have one son, Joseph Paul. They currently live at Cross Key near Hackneyville, Alabama. James has been self-employed since 1979. He has been a part-time local pastor with the North Alabama Conference of the United Methodist Church since June 2009 and is currently serving three churches in Clay and Talladega Counties. The churches are Shady Grove, Marvin Chapel and Sycamore. He would love to see you there one day. He preaches at each church each Sunday. He wants to preach at least once at Andrew's Chapel one day. God bless.

Perry G. Green

I was born near Sylacauga and moved to Hanover with my parents when I was very young. While I never lived in Goodwater it was near and my family traded there and I have had friends there for many years. I graduated from the rival high school and spent ten years, ten months, fourteen days, seven hours and twenty-six minutes in the USMC. I got to go on an all expenses paid trip to sunny South-East Asia for my Senior trip! I got out and went to school at UAB while serving in the Army National Guard. I finally graduated and spent almost ten years in the USAF and retired. While I still own the property and what's left of the old house in Hanover I currently live in Montgomery with a wife, two dogs and three birds. Had a rat with a sweet tooth that lived with us for about two years till I finally got the best of it, but that's another story! I spend my days drinking, telling lies, building dollhouses, spoiling a red-headed granddaughter and writing, not necessarily in that order!
I hope you have enjoyed these tales of a time long past but fondly remembered.